FESTIVE

Decorations

FESTIVE Decorations

MING VEEVERS–CARTER

OVER 80 DECORATIVE IDEAS FOR FLOWERS, WREATHS, AND TREES

Sterling Publishing Co., Inc.   New York

The publishers would like to thank the following for their
help and advice:

Old Jordans, Near Beaconsfield, Buckinghamshire
Owned and directed by The Religious Society of Friends
Old Jordans is set in a beautiful conservation area on a
site dating back to the late middle ages. The earliest recorded
date of the original farmhouse is 1618 and both the
Mayflower Barn and Dining Room, where photography took place,
are seventeenth century.

To my mother, Wendy,
thank you for all your love and time;
and to my daughter, Olivia.

Oasis is a registered trademark of Smithers Oasis Company

Published in 1990 by Sterling Publishing Company, Inc.
387 Park Avenue South, New York, N.Y. 10016

ISBN 0-8069-7474-5

Published in the U.K. under the title
Decorating with Nature by Merehurst Limited, London.
© 1990 by Merehurst Limited
This edition published by arrangement with
Merehurst Limited. Available in the United States,
Canada and the Philippine Islands only.
Distributed in Canada by Sterling Publishing
c/o Canadian Manda Group, P.O. Box 920, Station U
Toronto, Ontario, Canada M8Z 5P9

Library of Congress Cataloging-in-Publication Data

Veevers-Carter, Ming.
Festive decorations/Ming Veevers-Carter.
p. cm.
Includes index.
1. Flower arrangement. I. Title.
SB449.V45 1990
745.92—dc20   90–38847
CIP

2 4 6 8 10 9 7 5 3 1

Edited by Diana Brinton and Jane Struthers
Designed by Clare Finlaison
Jacket designed by Bridgewater Design
Photography by Jon Stewart, assisted by Kay Small
Styling by Barbara Stewart
Typeset by Rowland Phototypesetting Limited,
Bury St Edmunds, Suffolk
Colour separation by Fotographics Limited, London–Hong Kong
Printed in Italy by New Interlitho S.p.A., Milan

Contents

EQUIPMENT AND MECHANICS 8

DECORATING TREES 10

GARLANDS 24

WREATHS AND PLAQUES 46

CONE TREES 60

BALL TREES 76

FESTIVE TABLES 94

ARRANGEMENTS 110

CONSTRUCTED TREES 128

USEFUL TIPS 142

INDEX 143

AUTHOR'S ACKNOWLEDGMENTS 144

FOREWORD

Nearly a year after our wedding dance, guests were still phoning me to ask me the name of the florist. No-one there could ever forget that first sight of soaring bowers of pink and cream and green, nor the summery scent of lilies and roses on a cold November night. From the glorious table decorations to the delicacy of the napkins caught with tiny roses and ribbons, Ming Veevers-Carter's flowers personified the joy and happiness we felt on a very special day.

For me, this is the mark of a true florist: someone who can convey the spirit of the occasion and bring to it the human dimensions of warmth and pleasure. Ming allows flowers to speak for themselves. She decorates *with* nature, not against it.

Her flowers come together in combinations not always obvious but invariably harmonious. No-one is happier in the wee small hours of the morning at the flower market to come across something unexpected. Ming's mind immediately begins buzzing with ideas about how to incorporate it, and because of this her decorations always have a freshness. And they always have their own individual character, as she matches the personality of the flowers and arrangements to that of the occasion.

Ming can't imagine a day – especially days of celebration – without flowers, and after reading this book, there's no need for anyone, no matter how fumble-fingered, ever again to say 'I'd love to do something special, but I just don't know where to start . . .'

DEE NOLAN
Editor, Metropolitan Home

EQUIPMENT AND MECHANICS

Using the correct equipment and mechanics when making the arrangements shown in this book will not only make your task much easier but will also improve the appearance of the finished arrangements. A lot of the equipment will be very familiar, even if you are a newcomer to this type of flower arranging, but it is important to get used to some of the slightly more specialist items, such as oasis (floral foam).

Oasis

This is a plastic foam, rather like a sponge, and is designed to hold flowers and other materials in position. There are two basic forms – green oasis, which is water-retentive and can therefore be used with fresh materials, and brown oasis, which does not hold water and is intended for use with dried or artificial materials. Although green oasis may be left dry, it tends to crumble when used in this way, and it is better to select the brown variety for dry arrangements.

On the whole, I find that flowers drink better when directly in water, rather than oasis, and I tend to use 5cm (2in) wire netting to hold stems in position (see page 112), but for many of the specific arrangements featured here, oasis is essential. It comes in various forms: oasis blocks are the most usual shape, and can be cut and shaped, if necessary; oasis balls are ready-shaped balls, ideal for making ball trees; oasis rings are very useful for making advent rings and Christmas table decorations, and cones can be used to make small tree-shaped decorations.

Although I have used the name oasis throughout this book, because it is the word familiar to most people, it is in fact a brand name, and similar products can be found under various names.

Wires

A selection of wires are used for the majority of the decorations shown in this book: black and silver reel wires, and 0.71mm (22 gauge) and 1.25mm (18 gauge) stub wires. Use a separate container for your wires as it is essential to make sure that they are kept in a dry place at all times.

Oasis tape

This is used to hold oasis and other mechanics in place, so that your finished arrangement doesn't suddenly keel over. It should not be visible, but it is useful to have black, green and white, so that you can choose the least obtrusive colour.

Florists' scissors

These are specifically designed for cutting stems and wires, and are ideal for the job – as soon as you feel that you can justify buying a pair, it is a good idea to do so.

Plaster

This is essential for making ball trees and trees created from decorated branches. Ordinary plaster will do the job, but I generally use nylon reinforced plaster.

Gutta percha

This rubbery green tape is used to cover stub wires on wired flowers; for example, when making garlands.

The photograph shows a selection of the mechanics and equipment used to make the arrangements that are shown in this book.

1 Large and small watering cans – for topping up arrangements

2 Green florists' bucket – with side handles to avoid damaging flowers when the bucket is carried

3 Plant mister

4 5cm (2in) wire netting – for fresh flower arrangements

5 Plant pots

6 Black oasis tray

7 Nylon reinforced plaster

8 Ordinary plaster

9 Florists' scissors

10 Satin ribbon

11 Black and silver reel wires

12 Black and green oasis tapes

13 Gutta percha

14 Candle holders – for use with oasis rings, when making table arrangements

15 Silver stub wires

16 0.71mm (22 gauge) stub wires

17 1.25mm (18 gauge) stub wires

18 Green sticks

19 Green (wet) and brown (dry) oasis blocks

20 Oasis ring

21 Cylinder of oasis

22 Oasis cones

23 Oasis balls

24 Contorted willow

DECORATING TREES

The tradition of having a decorated pine tree as an obligatory part of the Christmas decorations came from Germany, after the marriage of Queen Victoria with Prince Albert. Once the Queen and her German husband had led the way, the rest of the people followed, and within a few years, the Christmas tree seemed more of an essential part of Christmas than the much older Anglo-Saxon tradition of the Yule log.

Christmas tree decorations are very much a matter of personal family taste and tradition, and it may be that if you want to depart from family tradition you will meet with considerable resistance. All the same, it is more exciting to get rid of the tatty old decorations, including that hairless old angel that has topped the tree for decades, and start afresh.

I used pearl beads to give a traditional swagging effect to this tree. The decorations are glass balls with glitter lattice work, frosty snow-flakes, three sets of gold lights, pearly gold baubles, cherubs and angels of frosted glass with golden wings.

There is an ever-increasing range of Christmas tree decorations, but it is often more effective to keep to about five different types; more tends to look untidy and lose impact.

Ribbon bows

To make a bow from satin ribbon, pull out a length of ribbon – this will be one of the tails of the bow, and should be about 10cm (4in) long, depending on the desired length of the tails. Holding this tail between your thumb and forefinger, make a loop, taking more ribbon from the reel; hold this loop, and make another, and continue, until you have as many loops as you want (four is the usual number). Twist a small length of silver reel wire around the centre, where you are holding the loops with your thumb and forefinger. Twist the wire on to itself and cut the ribbon.

Either choose a ready-wrapped parcel or an attractively patterned box. Wrap a length of ribbon around the parcel in the normal way, and tie a knot. Place your bow on the knot and tie a second knot over the bow concealing the wire and holding the bow in place. Trim the ends.

Decorative crackers

Decorative Christmas crackers are easy to make and are a quick and cheap form of decoration. They can be made any size, but the average size would be created by using an empty toilet roll or half a kitchen paper roll. Place the roll on the wrong side of a piece of wrapping paper; tape one edge of the paper to the cardboard, and then roll the paper around until the cardboard is completely wrapped, leaving a reasonable overlap at each end. Tape the free side in place, using either double-sided tape or clear tape.

Holding the wrapped roll in one hand, use the other hand to twist the paper close to the edge of the inner roll. Use a short length of black reel wire to hold the twist in place. Repeat at the other edge. Trim away any excess paper. The twist can be decorated with paper of another colour or with a bow. You may find that it is wise to warn children that these are purely decorative crackers, and there are no goodies inside – alternatively, let them help you to make the crackers in the first place.

Pot pourri parcels

To make pot pourri parcels, choose a soft fabric – silky lining fabric works well – of a colour to match your other tree decorations. Cut a square of fabric, approximately 25cm (10in) each way, then place two large handfuls of pot pourri in the centre. It is better to use the fine variety of pot pourri, rather than a very chunky type.

Gather up the material in one hand, holding it by its four corners. With the other hand, hold the material as close to the pot pourri as possible, so that it forms a round ball. Let go with the first hand, and twist the material slightly to keep it in place. Picking up one corner at a time, tuck the corners and raw edges in through the centre. Using a piece of black reel wire, secure the parcel by winding the wire around its neck. Finish by tying a bow over the wire. Alternatively, you can cut the fabric in a circle, using pinking shears, in which case you will not need to tuck in the edges.

RED AND GREEN TREE

If you want to be unrestrained, then this is the tree for you – it is Christmas, after all! To many people, red and green are the classic colours of Christmas, but it is a combination that can become predictable if you are not careful. Here, I used a mixture of red and tartan shop-bought bows, Victoriana balls, red artificial apples, pearly gold baubles, gold beads, cherubs, gold grapes, and golden baroque items that are not necessarily Christmassy in themselves, but which are very dramatic when used in this combination and create an exuberant, over-the-top atmosphere. The stockings reflect the colours of the rest of the tree and give it cohesion.

Firstly, put your lights in position on the tree, then wire a large cherub to the top of the tree, using 1.25mm (18 gauge) stub wires. Now garland the tree with the beads, looping them on to the branches with decoration hanging hooks. I find that it is best to use these hooks when you are hanging baubles or other decorations on a tree. The larger end, which is attached to the branch, should first be pinched between your thumb and forefinger to ensure that it will fit snugly when in place.

If you do not have these hooks, you can use silver stub wires instead. Whichever method you use, the effort is worth making – it seems such a waste if the decorations are not attached firmly to the tree, as they can easily fall off and break.

Using their own stems, twist the grapes on to the pine branches. Add all the other baubles and decorations. Finish by adding the cherubs and other baroque decorations, but first wire them with 0.71mm (22 gauge) wire, as the normal hooks would not be sufficiently strong.

This is a very festive, decorative tree, but you must be careful not to become over enthusiastic – a tree of this type will be more effective if the decorations are put on with a light touch. In fact, I'd suggest that you stand back from the tree every now and then while decorating it, and always make sure that it is pleasing to the eye before you add any more decorations. You can easily fill in any rather empty-looking patches later, if you decide that this is necessary.

This 2m (6ft 6in) tree was set in a 25cm (10in) diameter bucket filled with nylon reinforced plaster the night before it was decorated. The bucket was then draped in rich fabric.

IRON TREES

I think there is something very Shake-spearian about this setting – it reminds me of Macbeth and his castle at Cawdor! In the foreground you will see two hanging arrangements. I call these 'iron trees', and they were made especially for me, but as an alternative you could make large arrangements in hanging baskets which would look equally effective.

To do this, line each basket with a sheet of black plastic, then fill with three blocks of soaked green oasis covered with wire netting and secured to the top of the basket with black reel wire. Suspend each basket, using a heavy weight and preferably black chain, from a strong hook.

It is better to make this arrangement *in situ* as it is extremely heavy and difficult to move once it has been finished. Life will therefore be easier if you use a stepladder when creating the arrangement, and have a helper to pass things up to you. Arrange one side of the basket first, using fresh blue pine and also artificial frosty pine, holly and mistletoe, with perhaps a few trails of ivy to soften the effect, then move the stepladder and complete the other side. If you stretch over the basket you are likely to fall off the ladder!

The Christmas tree in the background contains clumps of mistletoe, candy cane, baubles and fairy lights, and has been garlanded with popcorn threaded with a needle and cotton: this is a good task to give to a child. The combination of the tree and the hanging arrangements creates a wonderful and highly evocative setting for any Christmas party.

BURGUNDY TREE

The impact of this tree belies the essentially straightforward way in which it has been decorated. It has two sets of lights, cream bows, burgundy bows, Victoriana papier mâché baubles and little coloured story books.

The burgundy bows are made from wired ribbon in exactly the same way as the bows of the Peach Bow Tree shown opposite, but the cream bows are made with satin ribbon. As you can see, the use of satin creates a completely different and much softer, glossy effect. Satin ribbon is easy to obtain, but wired ribbon, a recent arrival

on the market, can be a problem. I sell it in my shops, but very few other florists have followed this example, and you might find that you have to buy it in quantity – at least one full roll, which is some 25m (28yd) long. Alternatively, you might be able to obtain it through your local flower-arranging club. Having said this, wired ribbon is invaluable for decorations, and it is well worth hunting for a supplier.

To give a finishing touch, I placed a larger burgundy bow on the top of the tree to balance the shape and provide a focal point to the design.

PEACH BOW TREE

Bows offer a cheap and effective way of decorating a Christmas tree and have become quite popular over the last few years. Here, I used only one string of gold tree lights, but plenty of peach and brown bows, made from wired ribbon. This is the best ribbon to use, as it holds the shape of the bow perfectly.

Make the bows in two sections, as shown on page 12, using the middle section to secure the bow to the tree. Alternatively, you can make the bows and thread silver wire through their backs, using this to attach them to the tree. I don't, however, find that the wiring method is as secure as the ribbon ties.

If you find that it is completely impossible to obtain wired ribbon, you can make bows from stiffened fabric. The fabric can be stiffened either with fabric glue, or a thick paste of flour and water, or even with wood glue. Cut the fabric into strips 10cm (4in) wide; apply the stiffener and – while the fabric is still wet – fold the sides in to meet each other, so that you finish with a strip 5cm (2in) wide. Mould this into a bow while damp, and leave it to dry before you attach it to the tree.

LACE AND LIGHTS TREE

Although fresh pine Christmas trees are very attractive, they are not always suitable. For example, they may be too large for very small rooms, causing a rather claustrophobic atmosphere, or you may be going away for Christmas itself, in which case you are likely to return to a bald, dehydrated tree and a heap of needles on the floor. Artificial trees are very realistic these days, and are also easy to store, so you should have no difficulty in bringing them out year after year, if you wish.

When dressing the tree, put on the fairy lights first, followed by the chains of beads, which are twisted together in pairs to give a chunky effect. I then add paper flowers surrounded with lace, pomanders, bows and pearl gold baubles. Similar decorations to these can be bought in shops.

As this is an artificial tree, and therefore lacks the heady, Christmassy scent of fresh pine, the pomanders compensate to some extent by contributing their spicy tang to the tree (you might make your own pot pourri parcels, as shown on page 13). A bowl of a spicy seasonal pot pourri behind the tree also helps to evoke the scent of Christmas. Another trick is to put a few drops of concentrated pine oil here and there on the tree itself.

You could easily make lacy nosegays with small bunches of wired dried or artificial flowers, surrounded by a length of gathered lace. Take care when hanging these to place them where they will be seen from the right side and to position them well into the tree, so that they don't get damaged.

BLUE AND PINK TREE

This tree departs from the usual Christmas colours, yet it still looks very festive and special. Don't coordinate a scheme of this type too closely with the surrounding decor or your tree may end up looking a little like part of the furniture. An attractive and well chosen contrast will be more effective.

I used an artificial pine tree and then covered it with a few Father Christmas decorations, an angel, pearly beads, pink pot pourri parcels, blue bows and crackers – which you can make for yourself – and blue fairy lights.

Arrange the lights first, following this with the bead garlanding, and then add the other decorations.

Make the pot pourri parcels and crackers as shown in the steps on pages 12–13. For the parcels shown here, I used pink silk lining fabric, combining this with burgundy-coloured satin ribbon for the ties, which were formed into bows. The parcels can be attached to the tree with 0.71mm (22 gauge) stub wires.

The bows are made from blue satin ribbon 5cm (2in) wide, tied in the middle with burgundy ribbon, for added interest and to coordinate them with the pot pourri parcels. If you wish, the crackers can be decorated, perhaps with coloured ribbon or small pictures.

Beads have become a popular alternative to tinsel in recent years. They are readily available from Christmas supply shops and department stores, and you should have no difficulty in finding a colour that will coordinate with your scheme. You can use decoration hanging hooks to hold the loops, or else lay the string from branch to branch, as you would with tinsel. If your tree is likely to be ravaged by children – for example, if you have hung chocolate figures as a Christmas treat – you might find that it is safer to secure the bead loops in position with small pieces of silver reel wire.

For a final touch of colour coordination, you could wrap all your presents in the same paper that you used for the crackers, or – as here – choose two of the colours used for the tree. As the presents will be unwrapped on Christmas Eve or Day, you might wrap up a few extra, fake parcels, so that the bottom of the tree continues to look attractive throughout the twelve days.

GARLANDS

Garlands are a marvellously versatile form of decoration, especially when there is little or no available floor space, for example at a dance or a wedding party. They are a beautifully lavish way, for example, of decorating the staircase of a house that is to be used for a wedding reception or a coming-of-age party. Although they may appear to be a very extravagant way of using flowers and foliages, this need not necessarily be the case, for dried garlands are very long lasting, while artificial garlands can be used year after year.

On a small scale, a garland of fresh or dried flowers around the rim of a basket can revitalize it, and make it a charming receptacle for fruit, sweets or perhaps for pot pourri. A tiny garland around a champagne bottle makes it a very special gift, and shows that element of attention to small details that gives style to an occasion.

If you are giving a party in a very ornate or heavy setting, perhaps where there are large dark beams, or huge old fireplaces, then rather than using flowers, which might be too pretty and insubstantial for the setting, you might like to think of a rich conglomeration of exotic fruits and/or vegetables. Let your imagination run riot.

This basket is decorated with a garland formed from bunches of violets, attached individually to the edge with stub wires, as shown on the following page. It could be filled with edible goodies to be given as a gift or as a presentation at the end of a dinner party. Before you begin decorating the basket, place the bunches of violets in a sink full of water so that their heads are submerged, then leave them for at least two hours. This enables them to drink, as they absorb water better through their heads than their stems. Incidentally, they should not be left in water for more than 12 hours or they will rot. When you remove the violets from the water, dry them gently on a paper towel and cut the stems to about 5cm (2in) before arranging the bunches.

Garlanding a basket

Cut off the flower heads, leaving stems about
2.5cm (1in) long. Use large flowers singly but
gather small heads in twos or threes. Holding
the stem (or stems) between thumb and
forefinger, with the head towards your palm,
place a 0.71mm (22 gauge) stub wire at right
angles to the stem, close to the head and
overlapping the stem by about 2.5cm (1in) at
one side. Fold the short end down, then wind
the other around this and the stem, securing
them together. Hold one end of gutta percha
firmly to the top of the wired stem and twist,
using the other hand to pull down until the
entire length is covered.

Wire foliage in the same way as the flowers,
then start with a wired flower or bunch.
Holding it in one hand, take a second flower
or bunch and position this slightly below and
to the right of the first, twisting the second on
to the first; take a third flower or piece of
foliage and position this slightly below and to
the left. Twist this in place, then position the
next item at the centre, the following one to
the right, and so on. Cut all the excess wires
off approximately 5cm (2in) below the lowest
flower. Curve the garlanding around so that it
sits on the basket. Using a length of silver reel
wire, about 30 cm (12in) long, thread the wire
through the basket, feeding it between the
flowers. Pull tightly.

Another way of garlanding the edge of a
basket is to thread the wire to which the
flowers are attached directly through the
basket. Lay the flower heads flat on the rim
and take the remaining wire through the
basket a second time to secure them. This is
the best way to garland a basket if the
garlanding is heavy; for example, if you are
using cones, fruits or large flowers.

Fruit or vegetable garlands

When wiring fruit or vegetables, remember shapes and textures; for example, you can create an interesting effect by cutting a red cabbage in half. Peppers can be cut vertically or horizontally. Heavy items, such as cabbages or pineapples, can be mounted on two green garden sticks by pushing these through the bottom or the back, again varying this in order to add interest. The two legs will help to secure them so that they will not be swung around by their weight. For lighter items, use 1.25mm (18 gauge) stub wires, again pushing them through to make two legs.

To make the base for a fruit or vegetable garland, cut a strip of wire netting to the length of the object on to which you will be hanging the garland. Do not allow any extra for the drop, as the netting will stretch. Soak the oasis blocks and cut them into four pieces, cutting across the width. One block should be sufficient for approximately 60cm (24in) of garland. Place the oasis at equal intervals on the netting, leaving a gap of no more than 10cm (4in) between each block. Wrap the netting around the blocks and secure it on to itself as shown.

To hang the garland base, I suggest that you have someone to help you by taking up the slack while you secure the netting to the hook or nail with a 1.25mm (18 gauge) stub wire. Once both ends have been attached, place both hands palm down in the middle of the length and push down gently. This will stretch the netting. Always start adding the wired or mounted fruit to the garlanding in the middle and work evenly outwards towards the ends. If you wish to add greenery or flowers to fill gaps, leave these until the end, otherwise you will find that you obstruct the fruit from view and the garlanding will lose its impact. Be very careful not to overdo the flowers and/or foliage.

COVERED BASKET

An alternative to the traditional method of garlanding is to use a hot glue gun, available from good hardware stores. An old basket can be transformed into a decorative container for fruits, pot pourri, plants, or whatever else you might choose.

In this basket, we have used gold-rimmed black ribbon, dried rose and helichrysum heads, nuts, dried fungi, artificial berries and cones.

Each item has been glued in place individually, and it is easiest to work in small sections, filling in one area before you move on to the next. Instead of covering the entire outside of the basket, you might simply arrange dried flowers in loops around the outer edge of a basket. This is much quicker, and can look very charming. Start with a single flower at the top, and then work around the side, gradually increasing the depth of the decoration until you reach the centre of the loop, then reducing the depth as you work back to the top edge of the basket.

CHRISTMAS PINE GARLAND

This garlanding is made from wired blue pine, the pieces being linked on to each other in the same way as the flowers for the garlanded basket illustrated on page 26. This particular garland was made with 10cm (4in) pieces of pine on 1.25mm (18 gauge) stub wires.

To make a garland of this type, start by creating a plain garland of pine, and then add the baubles and bows as finishing touches. If you try to incorporate these into the garland as you make it, you will find that the baubles will get broken and the bows will be squashed. You might want to add other foliages, such as holly or ivy, or pine cones, or artificial fruits and berries, in which case it is best to incorporate these into the garlanding as you wire the pine pieces together. This creates a much more secure garland.

Normally, this type of garlanding would be hung along a mantelpiece, framing the fireplace, or on a wall, perhaps between two lights or pictures.

HYDRANGEA GARLAND

This is made in the same way as the Vegetable Garland (see page 27), but with brown oasis instead of green, as the hydrangeas are dried. It would be an ideal garland for decorating a hallway or kitchen, and its mellow colours are perfect for autumn or early winter.

I make a lot of use of hydrangeas, partly because their size makes them a useful cover for a large area. If you don't want to go to the trouble to make a garland, you will find that a basket filled with dried hydrangeas or a ball tree of hydrangea heads can make a luxurious decoration, perhaps at the side of a fireplace.

To make the garland, cut the stems of the hydrangeas about 10cm (4in) long and push them straight into the oasis – they will stay in place because the flower heads are so light. If you wish, you can twist a thin ribbon around the garland when it is finished. Alternatively, you might loop strips of fabric, strings of beads, or paper ribbon around the garland, to add to the rich, lavish effect.

Should you find it too expensive to buy all the dried hydrangeas needed to make this garland, you can easily dry fresh flower heads yourself. Pick them when the florets are fully open and firm to the touch, then hang them upside down individually in an airing cupboard or warm attic until dry – this should take about two weeks. Make sure that you dry many more than you think that you will need, as you will probably lose about one-third of them in the drying process. This is because, for no apparent reason, you will find that some of the heads shrivel as they dry out instead of holding their shape.

Like most dried flowers, the hydrangeas in this garland should last for about a year,

in normal conditions, before they lose their colour. When the hydrangeas start to look tired or faded, I find that it is very effective to spray them with a little pearl glitter to bring out their colours, but don't use too much or they will look gaudy. Although this garland looks very dramatic and attractive at its prime, it is an unfortunate fact that people tend to keep dried flowers for far too long. The glitter may prolong the life of the garland for a little while, but once the colours have really greyed and faded it is best to acknowledge the fact, and throw the garland away – in any case, if you have used flowers from the garden, the season should have come round again by the time the first garland is ready to be thrown out!

CHAMPAGNE GARLAND

This simple garland will give added impact to any special occasion, or can be used as an unusual way to gift-wrap a presentation bottle of champagne. Here, I used violets, muscari (grape hyacinths), sprays of rose leaves, eucalyptus, cream hyacinth bells and moss roses.

All the flowers were wired as shown in the first step on page 26. They were wired individually, with the exception of the violets. These are small and fragile and are therefore better left in groups. Cover all the wired stems with gutta percha. Measure the area around which you wish to place the garland, using a 1.25mm (18 gauge) stub wire, then bind the ends of the wire together to make a circle to use as a base and cover this with gutta percha.

Starting at one end and holding your hand on the inside of the circle, twist the flower stems on to it until it is completely covered, then gently drop it over the neck of the champagne bottle just before you present it.

CHRISTMAS BASKET

This basket, with its garland of golden fruit and nuts, is an attractive decoration, whether used on its own or as a festive way of transporting presents on Christmas Day.

I used a mixture of gold tree decorations and gold bows, combined with walnuts and pine cones. To gild the latter, first wire the pine cones and walnuts with 0.71mm (22 gauge) stub wires, then cover them with gold paint. This is a rather laborious process and very messy, but I do like the finished effect.

Alternatively, you can use a can of gold paint, which is certainly much easier and less time-consuming. To use the spray method, push the wires into a block of oasis, which you have first placed on a large sheet of plastic to protect your work surface; spray the cones and nuts from overhead, and allow them to dry. When they have dried, remove each pine cone and nut from the oasis in turn; hold the bottom of the wire in one hand; spray the base, then replace it in the oasis and leave until dry.

Starting with the long, golden decorations, place them at strategic intervals around the top of the basket, securing each one with a 0.71mm (22 gauge) stub wire that has been passed through the side of the basket, twisted around itself, cut off, and bent back towards the basket. Then add the pine cones, walnuts, gold grapes and finally the bows, wiring them in place in the same way as the other decorations.

NAPKIN GARLAND

Garlands of this type can be made from virtually anything, whether fresh, dried or artificial, but each item must be wired individually and the stems then covered with gutta percha.

Measure three-quarters of the circumference of the napkin when rolled up, using 1.25mm (18 gauge) stub wire, and cut the wire to that length. Cover the length of wire with gutta percha and then shape it to fit the rolled-up napkin snugly.

Leaving it in this shape, slide it off the napkin and begin to wire the garland. Here, I used silver pine cones, walnuts and artificial pine. It is not a good idea to fill the entire circle as the decorations beneath the

napkin will either be crushed or will make it unbalanced. Once you have completed the garland, fit it on to the napkin ring and ensure that it is easy to remove.

EASTER GARLAND

This flower garland, filled with Easter eggs and sugared almonds, in colours chosen to complement the flowers, makes a lovely table decoration or centrepiece, but don't be surprised if the chocolate eggs soon vanish, as they look very tempting when arranged like this!

As this garland is intended to be placed on a table, it should be flexible, but it does not need to be very strong or self-supporting, so the flowers can be bound on to each other. Here, I used white ranunculi, muscari, pink roses, moss roses, violets and green ivy leaves. The size of the Easter eggs could easily outweigh that of the flowers, so group the muscari, moss roses and violets in clumps to give them more density.

Wire the flower stems with thick silver stub wires, cover them with gutta percha, and then bind them on to each other to form a circle. The gutta percha will protect your table from scratches, but if you don't want to cover all the stems, you could place the garland on a tray, or perhaps attach it to a basket.

KUMQUAT GARLAND

If you wish to decorate a large salver for a buffet party, this garland of kumquats, blue pine, walnuts, brazil nuts and pine cones will certainly be a good talking point, and will also look most unusual.

To make it, wire all the individual items with 0.71mm (22 gauge) wires. Wire the kumquats by pushing the wire through from one side to the other, then bending the two protruding ends to form right angles to the fruit. Cover all the wired stems with gutta percha, then twist them on to each other. The finished garland will not be very strong, but it will be supported by the salver.

Remember to line the dish with lettuce leaves or something similar, to protect the food from pine needles.

VEGETABLE GARLAND

Perfect for decorating the kitchen at an informal party, a vegetable garland is quite unusual but can look absolutely stunning, especially if you choose a mixture of glossy and textural vegetables. Of course, it may seem very wasteful, and to some people, the idea of using good food in this way may be appalling – even immoral – but really it is no more expensive and wasteful than an arrangement of fresh flowers – in fact, it might be a lot cheaper. And for that matter, some of the flowers that I frequently use are also edible!

Depending on how long the garland is in position, you can in fact finish by eating your arrangement, providing you don't use the parts that have lengths of wire in them.

Here, I used leeks, red cabbages, cauliflowers, red peppers, squash, lettuces, artichokes, aubergines, celery and fatsia seeds. So that they would sit better on the garland and look more attractive, I cut the peppers in half crossways, the leeks and celery lengthways, and the red cabbage into quarters. The cabbages, cauliflowers, artichokes and aubergines had to be supported with garden sticks.

When you think of the weight of a loaded shopping basket, you will appreciate that a garland of this type is extremely heavy, and you will certainly need to make sure that it is very securely hung. The oasis will continue to drip water for about half an hour after the garland base has been hung, so if the floor is carpeted or of highly polished wood you will be very unpopular unless you first protect it with plastic sheeting. You will also need a covered work surface, a chopping board, and a sharp kitchen knife.

The fireplace seen here is about 2m (6ft 6in) wide, and the arrangement took me well under an hour to make, but I have had the advantage of about ten years' experience in making this type of garland. If this is your first attempt, it would be sensible to set aside at least two hours if you are making a garland this size – the next time you will probably find you can do it much more quickly. The good news is that it can be made up to half a day in advance of the party and will still look fresh, provided that you spray it regularly with water from a mister or a flower spray.

SUMMERY GARLAND

By using only flowers – 'La Rêve' lilies, 'Evelyn' roses, moss roses, cow parsley and white campanulas – for this garland, it has been given a very light and floral look. An enormous variety of flowers could be used for this garland, so if you have a flourishing garden you could almost pick at will. If you have an abundance of one particular type of flower, such as sweet peas, you could use this exclusively, perhaps padding it out with foliage. If you don't want to strip your garden bare – or this would cause a family argument of outsize proportions – you could make a very beautiful summery garland simply with cow parsley, or Queen Anne's lace, and a scattering of roses, lilies, or some other striking flower.

If the flowers are to appear at their best and stay fresh, they must be well prepared first. Bash the stems of the cow parsley, then put it in a bucket containing 5cm (2in) of boiling water and leave it to stand for not less than 10 minutes. After this, put the cow parsley in another bucket, this time filled with cold water, and leave it to drink for at least a day.

All the other flowers should be left in water for at least a good 12 hours before they are arranged, as this will prolong their lives. Also, you will very often find when you buy or pick flowers that they tend to be tighter than necessary, so if you give them a long drink this will encourage the petals to open slightly.

To make the garland, wrap small pieces of soaked green oasis in a tube of wire netting, as for the Vegetable Garland (see pages 36–7). This will keep the garland fresher, but it should only be hung on a wall or trellis, or used flat, because it will be too heavy to be pinned to a tablecloth or anything similar. If you are hanging a fresh flower garland outside – to decorate a patio for a party, for example – try to choose a shady and protected wall. Depending on the mixture of flowers, a garland of this type should last at least 12 hours, and it will probably last for 24 hours before some of the flowers will begin to fade. With this in mind, it would be wisest to make it no more than three hours before a party.

ARTIFICIAL GARLAND

This garland is made in exactly the same way as the Dried Garland on the following page. Artificial flowers are much more hard-wearing than their fresh or dried counterparts, which is particularly useful if they will be used to decorate tables where people might brush against them.

If you are making this garland for a table at which guests will be sitting, only put the garlanding along the vacant sides or it will be in the way. Normally, in any case, this type of garlanding would be used to decorate a buffet table, or perhaps the front of a bridal table.

If you are unsure about the length of garland that you will actually need, I would suggest that you make several lengths, each between 1 and 1.3 metres (3 and 4 feet) long. It will then be easy to join them together to make whatever length you require, using green garden twine or wire covered with gutta percha to make the joins. Alternatively, if the garland is to be arranged in loops, you might make the lengths long enough for one or two loops, and cover the joins with bows.

If your garland is too long, on the other hand, you will find that it is very difficult to cut it in half, as it will tend to disintegrate.

Artificial flowers are mounted on wired stems, but you should replace these with stub wires as the wired stems are so thick that they will not sit properly or entwine successfully on the green garden twine, and the end result will be a very thick, stiff, unattractive garland.

The flowers used for this garland are white roses, lilac and hydrangeas, and some artificial plums were added to give extra interest and a luscious, rich effect to the combination.

The garland shown here is thick and luxurious, but you could, of course, make a narrower garland and bulk it out by winding it around ropes of trailing ivy. Alternatively, you might add individual flowers to a garland of smilax. Both these alternatives would be time-consuming, however, and you would have to make the garland on the wedding day itself. In any case this would lose the advantage of using artificial flowers.

DRIED GARLAND

The muted colours of this dried garland make it a very pretty decoration for a party. Dried flowers have to be treated with care if they are to stay at their best so, if you wish this garland to be a permanent fixture in a room, do not place it in direct sunlight or anywhere that is damp.

This dried garland was made from hydrangeas, amaranthus, roses, larkspur, clover and marjoram. When using dried flowers with small heads they will look best if wired in groups of five. Wire the bunches with thin silver wire, then cover the stems with gutta percha. Measure the distance you wish to cover with green garden twine, remembering to allow for the downward curve of the garland rather than just measuring straight across. Always allow an extra 12–15cm (5–6in) for the loops at each end and the slack that is taken up when the dried flowers are wired on. It is better to wire all the way round these garlands rather than only the front, otherwise the weight of the flowers will distort the garland and reveal the mechanics at the back. Tie a loop at each end before you start, then place the first bunch of dried flowers close to one of the loops and twist the guttaed wires round and round the string. Continue doing this along the string until you reach the other loop, keeping the flowers tightly grouped to protect them and to retain the shape of the garland.

If you wish to attach the finished garland to a tablecloth, it is best to use long dressmaking pins at each corner and also to place one in the centre of the garland for additional support.

FRUIT GARLAND

This is a variation on the theme of the Vegetable Garland, on pages 36–7, but using just a selection of the marvellous fruits that are now readily available in many supermarkets, including grapes, apples, Cape gooseberries, South African pears, plums, melons, mini bananas, strawberries, kumquats and passion fruits. These last are best used whole, if at all; if you cut a passion fruit in half, the inside will quickly become shrivelled and dull-looking.

Of course, you can also use flowers and foliage (here, I used proteas), to lighten the effect, both visually and literally, of all those fruits. Indeed, it is important to bear in mind that the combined weight of the fruits can be very considerable in a garland of this type, so make sure it is secure.

Most of the fruits were pinned to the garland with 1.25mm (18 gauge) stub wires, but the strawberries and softer fruits were pinned on to the other fruits rather than the oasis, using 0.71mm (22 gauge) wires – anything thicker would have torn their soft flesh.

The immense weight of this garland makes it an unsuitable decoration for a tablecloth, as it must be put in a place that can offer the necessary support. You must also remember when siting it that fruit juices will almost inevitably ooze out and may cause permanent stains – on wallpaper, for example.

GARLANDED FIREPLACE

When using purchased artificial garlanding, it is very important to open it out fully, because it usually becomes rather squashed in packing. Fortunately, as all the stems are wired and very pliable, the garlanding is easy to bend and shape.

You will often find that you will need to use two garlands, twisting them around each other to create a really full, rich effect. You might decide simply to wind two garlands of the same type together, or alternatively you might combine a garland of cones with one of pine.

Although the idea of artificial garlanding may not instantly appeal to you, it has several advantages over garlanding made from fresh materials. Falling needles can be a nuisance, and a fresh garland will tend to shed needles all the faster if it is hung over a fireplace. Another advantage of using an artificial garland, of course, is that you can re-use it almost indefinitely, provided you look after it properly. Store it in a cardboard box, and remember to remove any decorations before you pack it.

Hang the garland in position before you add any decorations. Here, I hammered two small nails into the fireplace surround and attached the garland to them with black reel wire so that there was a garland across the fireplace and swags hanging down either side. Do make sure that the garland is very secure before you add any

further decorations, and don't forget that these will increase the weight of the garland. On the other hand, one of the advantages of an artificial garland is that it weighs considerably less than a garland of fresh pine, and it is therefore only necessary to use small nails, whereas for a fresh garland you would need much larger nails.

There is no need to incorporate a great many extra decorations – I used a few gold bows, cherubs, gold bunches of grapes, baubles, golden baroque hanging decorations, and golden pine cones, holding them all in place with 0.71mm (22 gauge) stub wires. If you will be lighting a fire in the grate, you must ensure that the garland is well out of the way of any heat or of sparks that might fly out, as artificial foliage is more flammable than the fresh variety. It is also a sensible precaution to spray it before use with fire-retardant, which is available from good hardware stores.

Another attractive place for a garland of this type is around a window, particularly one that is left uncurtained, perhaps because of its decorative shape. Alternatively, you might use it to frame a doorway, archway or alcove. Hammer small nails around the area to be gathered, then wire the garland in position with silver stub wires, adding any further decorations when the garland is *in situ*, as for a fireplace garland.

WREATHS AND PLAQUES

Like garlands, wall plaques are an ideal decoration for a bare wall or for a pillar and, once again, they keep the floor clear for guests at a party. They have the added advantage at a dance or party that they can be placed high up, where they will be seen, while an arrangement at eye level will often be obscured as soon as the room starts to fill up. I often make very large wall plaques, up to 2 metres (6–7 feet) across, but these require a lot of mechanics. Smaller plaques, up to a metre (3 feet) across, are relatively easy to handle and in fact I find them easier than standing designs, because you are effectively working on two dimensions rather than three. That said, you must be careful to check at each side of a finished arrangement, to make sure that it lies flush with the wall and there are no visible mechanics.

Wreath is perhaps an unfortunate word for a circular arrangement with a hole in the middle, as it may have funereal connotations, but it is a type of arrangement that offers endless possibilities. We tend to think in terms of Christmas wreaths, but they can make a very attractive wall arrangement for any season; for example, nut wreaths in autumn, fresh or artificial flowers for a summery feel, or perhaps a maypole-type design to celebrate the first of May.

This nut wreath is a wonderful way to celebrate Harvest-time or even Thanksgiving, with its mixture of warm browns provided by the unshelled walnuts, brazil nuts, peanuts and hazelnuts that have been used. The base of the wreath was a ready-made lavender ring, which offered a good solid frame on which to work and gave out wafts of delicious scent. I used a hot glue gun to attach the nuts, starting with the larger nuts and then filling in with the peanuts and hazelnuts. If you are making a wreath of this type, remember to leave a space of about 7.5cm (3in) at the top for a lavish bow to give the perfect finishing touch.

Plaques

To make a plaque, start by taking a block of oasis. If you are making a fruit and/or flower plaque and will be using fresh materials, use soaked green oasis; otherwise use brown oasis. One block of oasis will make a flower plaque approximately 60cm (24in) each way (a fruit plaque will be slightly larger than the oasis). If you wish to put two blocks together, I suggest that you use green garden sticks to join them, and if the plaque is to be very large, it would be best to mount it on a wooden base. Start by placing the oasis on a piece of wire netting.

Wrap the netting around the oasis, and secure it on to itself. It is advisable to thread a 1.25mm (18 gauge) stub wire through the netting join to make it doubly secure. Join the netting along the underneath of the block and at both ends. Thread another 1.25mm (18 gauge) stub wire through one end of the netting and twist it on itself to form a loop from which the oasis will hang. Cut a piece of black plastic – from a dustbin bag, for example – making it approximately 5cm (2in) larger than the block. Place the oasis block, seam down, on the plastic; fold the edges of the plastic in towards the block, and pin them in place, using small lengths of 1.25mm (18 gauge) stub wire. The plastic will stop the oasis from rubbing and leaving damp marks.

Advent rings

Oasis rings can be purchased, complete with plastic bases. The best way of soaking these is to turn them upside down in a basin of water. Once the ring is fully soaked – this will take approximately 10 minutes – place your candle holders evenly into the oasis. It is important to use these as you will probably want to change your candles more than once in the life of an advent ring, and the holders will enable you to do this without crushing the oasis. Cut tips of pine (blue pine was used here) approximately 7.5–10cm (3–4in) long, and strip the needles from the bottom 2.5cm (1in) of the stem.

Push lengths of pine into the ring, positioning them at an angle of approximately 45 degrees. The angle at which the pine is inserted is very important, as it is essential to cover all the oasis, allowing none to remain visible. Remember that guests will be looking down on the arrangement, so if the pieces stick upright, they will not be fully appreciated. Once you have inserted all your pine, then – and not before – you can start adding the extras, such as nuts, cones and baubles. The candles are the last things to be added.

To wire cones for use in arrangements, use 1.25mm (18 gauge) stub wires unless the cones are very small, in which case 0.71mm (22 gauge) wires will be sufficient. The wire is looped through the bottom kernels of the cone and is then tightly twisted on to itself. For walnuts, dip one end of a 1.25 mm (18 gauge) stub wire into an all-purpose glue and then stick it up the bottom of the nut. For harder nuts, such as pecans and brazil nuts, you will have to drill a small hole before you can insert the wire. To wire pine, first strip off the bottom needles, then turn one end of a stub wire back and lay the flattened loop against the stem. Twist the longer end around the wire and stem, as shown.

Door wreaths

To make a door wreath, I suggest that you buy a circular wreath ring. These are available in a wide range of sizes; the pine will extend the diameter of the ring by approximately 10cm (4in). Start by placing a piece of wired pine flat along the frame. Hold it in place by gripping the end of the stem with the thumb and forefinger of one hand and use the other hand to twist the wire around the frame. Always twist the wires in the same direction, for a smoother and more secure finish. Add holly, nuts and other decorations as you work around the frame.

SUMMER
ARTIFICIAL WREATH

This wreath makes an ideal centrepiece for a table or decoration for a wall, and can be made from fresh flowers instead of the artificial materials shown here, though the latter will, of course, last much longer.

When making wreaths with artificial flowers it is important not to choose any that are too large and are out-of-scale with the others, as they will only look heavy in the finished arrangement. Although I used a hydrangea head, I split it into florets. Arrange the dog roses first, followed by the spray roses, lilac, berries, hydrangea florets and little purple campanulas. I think that it is important to keep wreaths of this sort tight and full, otherwise you will be able to see the oasis.

If you wish to make this wreath with fresh flowers, you must soak a green oasis ring in water. When making a fresh wall decoration, I would strongly suggest that you make it flat, then hang it in position at least two hours before it will be needed, as water will dribble from the oasis.

HANGING MAYPOLE DECORATION

This is a very pretty arrangement for midsummer parties and, if the bottom of the pole is set into plaster, can be used as a decoration above a table, on the corners of dance floors, or as a free-standing arrangement, in a house or garden.

It is made on a soaked ring of green oasis that has been suspended from the top of the pole with lengths of green-coated garden wire. I would suggest that you position the wires at four evenly-spaced points around the ring, taking great care to make sure that they are all of equal length, so that the ring hangs evenly. The wires will later be covered by ribbons.

When you have suspended the ring, you can then make the arrangement *in situ*, which is the only way to ensure that it looks right. Here, I used hydrangeas, blue bee, camomile daisies, parrot tulips, 'Lovely Girl' roses, 'Champagne' roses, white ranunculas and white blossom. Hide the wires by draping prettily-coloured ribbons downwards from the top of the pole.

CHRISTMAS DOOR WREATH

Fill your guests with Christmas cheer when they arrive by decorating your front door with a festive wreath. It is relatively simple to make and highly effective. If you can also arrange a fresh fall of snow, then so much the better!

For this wreath I used blue pine, plastic holly, red apples, pine cones and nuts, all of which were wired with 0.71mm (22 gauge) wires, with the exception of the apples, for which 1.25mm (18 gauge) wires were used. I chose a ready-made wire ring for the base of the wreath. Start arranging the foliage and decoration on one side of the wire ring and work your way round, leaving a small area, approximately 5cm (2in) wide, for the bow. This can be placed at the top or the bottom of the wreath, according to your design. There is no need to cover the wired stems with gutta percha as they will never be seen. If you wish to place the wreath on a glass door, remember to make it completely round rather than flat, otherwise the mechanics will be visible through the glass. When creating a wreath, as with any other type of garland, keep the items close together to stop any movement that might occur.

HANGING PINE ADVENT RING

If you have wooden beams in your house then why not bring attention to them over Christmas with a hanging advent ring (overleaf)? If you wish to use the advent ring in the traditional way, you should light the first candle on the first Sunday in Advent, continuing to light another candle on the next and following Sundays, finally lighting the fourth candle on Christmas Day.

Soak a green oasis ring in water, then cut four pieces of tartan ribbon long enough to allow your arrangement to hang in the correct position. Place the candle holders in the oasis and tie each piece of ribbon securely and evenly around the oasis ring, then hang it in position. Place the candles, still in their plastic wrappers, in the candle holders, then cover the oasis ring completely with tips of blue pine, from which the lower needles have been removed. Next, wire each artificial red apple with a 1.25mm (18 gauge) stub wire; do this by heating one end over a candle flame, then pushing it through the bottom of the apple to hold it securely inside. Now arrange the apples around the ring, followed by a little plastic mistletoe, and the nuts and cones which should all be wired on 0.71mm (22 gauge) wires. Lastly, remove the plastic candle wrappings.

WINTER FIREPLACE ARRANGEMENT

The texture and colouring of pine cones makes them marvellous as decorations for autumn and winter – they look so seasonal and interesting. The trees shown here are made by pushing small cones of brown oasis on to short straight branches. These can either be set in pots of reinforced nylon plaster or nailed to a few tiny logs.

Wire each pine cone with a 0.71mm (22 gauge) stub wire. When you have done this, push them into the oasis, starting at the bottom of each oasis shape and, keeping the pine cones as evenly spaced as possible, working round and round until you reach the top.

The wreath is made from a wire ring, on to which the pine cones are wired. To ensure that the cones stay in place, put a spot of glue at each place where they touch, to hold them together. You will find that it is easiest to do this if the wreath is laid flat on a work surface. Once the glue is dry and you are sure that the pine cones are fixed firmly in place, you can loop a wire to the back of the wreath and hang it on the wall above the fireplace.

PINE AND NUT BALLS

If you wish to decorate a door or wall but want a change from the classic wreath, this is a good option. It is made from blue pine, pine cones and walnuts, and is particularly suitable for autumnal and Christmassy occasions.

Slice a block of wet green oasis in half to make two bases, each 2.5cm (1in) deep, on which to work. Cut off the sharp corners of one to make a rough circle and wrap it in wire netting. Line the back with a piece of plastic, securing it to the sides of the oasis with pins made from 0.71mm (22 gauge) wire. Repeat for the other circle, making it half the size of the first one.

Using tips of blue pine not more than 7.5cm (3in) long, from which the lower needles have been stripped, insert them into the oasis, starting from the outer circle and working in towards the middle. Attach the small ball to the main one with a 0.71mm (22 gauge) wire, then cover it with a piece of ribbon which you have wired at each end so that it can be stuck into the oasis at these points. Wire the cones and nuts with 0.71mm (22 gauge) wires and place them in the arrangement. Make two bows, thread a 0.71mm (22 gauge) wire through the back of each one and push it into the top of each ball.

FRUIT PLAQUE

As fresh fruit is highly perishable, it is best to make this plaque (overleaf) no more than two or three hours before it is needed. The dramatic swags of fabric behind it give added impact and make the perfect background against which to display the different colours of the fruits.

To make the plaque, place two blocks of wet green oasis on a sheet of 5cm (2in) wire netting and wrap it securely round them, twisting the ends together. Then, for added security, 'stitch' the join together with a 0.71mm (22 gauge) stub wire. Cover the back of the netting with a piece of black plastic, then attach it to the oasis with 0.71mm (22 gauge) pins. Now run a 1.25mm (18 gauge) stub wire through one end of the wire netting parcel – this will be used to attach the oasis to a strong nail, fixed to the wall. Wire the bottom of the parcel in the same way.

Before you put in any fruit, arrange the swags of material on the wall. You can then begin work on the plaque. Here, I arranged the bananas and grapes first, followed by the smaller fruit: apples, nectarines, plums and kumquats. Half an hour before the plaque was needed I sliced some kiwi fruits in half and added them: any earlier, and they would have dried out by the time the guests arrived. The table centrepiece was made from a pyramid of wet green oasis covered with wire netting, into which the fruit was wired.

VALENTINE HEART

To make this Valentine heart, gather a good handful of sphagnum moss, then squeeze it into as neat a package as possible. Take a reel of black wire, then stick one end of the wire into the centre of the moss package, and tightly wrap the wire round and round the moss until it is secure. Once you have a firm base from which to work, keep adding more moss, wrapping it round with wire, until you have made a compact heart shape of the required size. Place the heart on a piece of black or clear plastic and cut around the shape. Then, using pins made from 0.71mm (22 gauge) wires, attach the plastic to the moss. This will enable you to place the heart on a table or other surface without damaging it.

Choose flowers with small heads, as larger flowers make it difficult to maintain the heart shape. Ensure that the flowers and their stems are no more than 5cm (2in) long. For this heart, I used fresh red moss roses and muscari, wiring the individual flowers on to thick silver wires. Once the flowers are all wired, cut off the wires about 2.5cm (1in) below the stems.

CONE TREES

This type of constructed tree has become a very fashionable design accessory, and fits particularly well into the more stream-lined type of modern home. A major advantage is that it can be shaped to take very little space; Christmas trees can be made to fit into a narrow space or a difficult corner, for example. Cone trees can be tiny, designed for use as side or dinner table decorations, or they may be up to 2 metres (7 feet) tall, and in theory they could be even taller, though this would be a time-consuming option.

I make a lot of the smaller trees, as I find that they give me a chance to escape from traditional ways of using flowers, and a small flower tree creates a lot of interest and can make an impact out of proportion to its small size.

If you are giving a dinner party and have a great deal of cutlery, glasses, side dishes and so on to fit on the table, a cone tree will generally take up far less space than almost any other type of arrangement. This is a particularly valuable option at Christmas-time, when the hostess is often faced with the problem of accommodating more guests than she really has room for.

This conical tree of blue pine, artificial holly and artificial pine is hand-made, using the method shown in the third and fourth steps on pages 62–3, and would be ideal for a small area for which a normal, spreading Christmas tree would be too wide or too elaborate. In this case, I started with twigs of blue pine. These were graded in length from 60cm (24in), at the bottom of the tree, to no more than 20cm (8in) at the top. Next, the partridges were attached securely to the netting with 1.25mm (18 gauge) stub wires, then the artificial pine and holly were added. The plastic pears were wired on with 1.25mm stub wires. To do this, you need to heat one end of the wire in a candle flame, then push it through from one end of the pear to the other. Bend the two ends of the wire into a hairpin shape and push them into the netting. A few baubles complete the decorations.

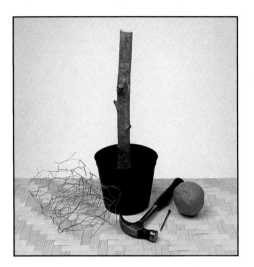

Making cone trees

For a cone tree, choose a branch for the trunk of the tree, and put it into a flower pot three-quarters full of plaster or nylon reinforced plaster. Leave it to dry, which will take about an hour for ordinary plaster or 24 hours for the nylon reinforced variety, which is heavier and cleaner to handle. The height and thickness of the branch are important, because the trunk must have the correct visual balance and be strong enough to act as a support.

To make a fruit and flower pyramid, wrap half, quarter or full blocks of soaked oasis in wire netting. Hammer securing nails into the trunk: one at the top, then one a little under each oasis block. If, for example, you are making a large all-round pyramid, you will have three blocks of oasis suspended from the top nail; then there will be three or four nails below these blocks, to hold the next layer of blocks, and so on. To attach each oasis block, thread a 1.25mm (18 gauge) stub wire through the netting and twist it on to the nail; thread a second wire through the bottom end of the block and twist this around the trunk. To make doubly sure that they do not swing, the blocks can be wired to each other.

To make a conical pine or box tree, hammer a strong nail into the top of the pole. Take 5cm (2in) gauge wire netting and crunch and roll this into the approximate size and shape of the cone. Push it on to the pole. Secure the netting to the top nail with a 1.25mm (18 gauge) stub wire. If there are loose, shaky areas, link different areas with stub wires to make the construction more solid. Tuck excess netting into the pot. Attach black reel wire to the netting, just above the pot, passing the wire under the pot, pulling it tightly, and securing it to the netting on the other side. Repeat on the opposite side of the pot, twisting the second wire on to the first as you pass it under the pot, to prevent slipping.

Use either blue pine or boxwood to make your base. For a 90cm (3ft) high tree, the bottom lengths of pine or box should be no longer than 35cm (14in). When cutting your pieces, do not trim away the side branches as these will help to keep the lengths in place. When inserting pine or box into the netting structure, push them in towards the central pole at right angles. Do this all the way around, then shorten the lengths a little for the layer above. The end product should be full, so that no wire netting or other mechanics are visible. Add any decorations once the basic cone is complete.

To make a small cone of pine, cut tips of pine approximately 10cm (4in) long and strip the bottom needles. Push the stems into the oasis cone. These cones can only be bought in brown oasis. If you wish the pine to keep fresh for longer, carve a cone shape out of a block of soaked green oasis and place the bottom of the cone into a jam jar lid. This will protect your table or other surface from water stains.

To make a dried flower cone, place a dry oasis cone into a suitable pot – it should ideally fit snugly into the pot. To make sure that the oasis is secure, you can glue it into position with an all-purpose glue, or you can cover it with wire netting, securing this to your bowl with oasis tape. When making a cone of this type, I suggest that you put the largest flowers in first, as these will give you a basic outline with which to work.

GERMAN GINGERBREAD TREE

This handsome pine Christmas tree is ideal for a child's bedroom or playroom, as it is quite solid and rather fun. It also, of course, has edible decorations, which usually appeal to children of all ages, adding greatly to its attraction!

This is made like the conical pine tree on pages 62–3, using blue pine and filling in the shape all round. If you bake your own gingerbread men, you may find it easiest to hang them if you make tiny ribbon bows, like neckties, twist silver wire around these – behind the necks of the gingerbread men – make another twist, and then attach the ends to the blue pine. You should also use silver wire to attach all the other decorations to the tree, because you will find that if you try to hang them by their own loops they will just slip off.

Other edible decorations include bags of gold chocolate money (a good, traditional favourite), little wrapped chocolate parcels, or even individually-wrapped sweets. Bags of miniature bars and tiny boxes of sweets are readily available from most supermarkets, and can be wrapped in shiny paper to make attractive small parcels. Use narrow ribbon to hang them from the trees. You can also buy or make miniature baskets and fill them with sweets. If you were making a small-scale tree as a table decoration, you could add marzipan fruits or other after-dinner treats.

An edible tree of this type is great fun, but it can end up looking rather sad and depleted, so it is important to have a store of replacement goodies, to fill in the gaps as they occur.

This is chiefly a children's tree, so moveable wooden toys would make an added attraction, as would tiny teddy bears and story books. Perhaps the toys could be handed out when the tree is finally dismantled at the end of the Christmas period, providing some much-needed consolation for the end of the holiday!

MINIATURE TREES

These little trees are perfect table decorations for Christmas Day, and make a refreshing change from the usual long table arrangements. If you wish to give a feeling of continuity to the rest of your decorations, you can make them as miniature versions of your main tree.

To make each tree, take a block of green oasis that has been soaked in water, and place in a basket lined with black plastic. To fit the block into the basket, you will have to trim a little off the bottom with a sharp kitchen knife. Once the oasis is in place, shape the top part into a cone with the knife, but do remember to place a large plastic sheet beneath the basket to catch the small pieces of oasis that fall off as you trim them. Now take tips of sugar pine, cut them into 10cm (4in) lengths and strip off the lower needles, leaving about 2.5cm (1in) of bare stem. Begin to insert them into the oasis, starting from the bottom of the cone and working your way round until you reach the top. Place the final pieces of pine, vertically, at the top.

Next arrange the silver beads, used to garland the trees, holding them in place with pins of 0.71mm (22 gauge) wire. Now make the small red bows from ribbon, thread 0.71mm (22 gauge) stub wires through their backs and pin in place. Do not overdo the bows – seven or nine to a tree should be enough. If you wish to keep these trees alive for more than a few days, remove the bows and gently water them from overhead, or spray them with a plant mister and leave on a draining board overnight, replacing the bows in the morning.

PINE AND TARTAN TREE

Christmas trees come in many shapes and sizes, as you can see from this Pine and Tartan Tree. It is a good choice if you want a traditionally coloured Christmas decoration, but with a difference. As well as blue pine, this hand-made tree incorporates artificial currants, walnuts and tartan bows.

Follow the instructions given for the conical pine tree on pages 62–3, but only decorate three-quarters of the main branch, to enable it to be placed relatively far back into the corner. Wire the nuts on 1.25mm (18 gauge) stub wires, bunch them into groups of two or three, then push the wires through the netting. Use silver reel wire to attach the tartan bows to the blue pine. Leave the artificial currants on their original stems; these can easily be pushed through the wire netting, which will hold them firmly in place.

FRUIT AND FLOWER TREE

The sharp, clear colours of this little tree make it a good choice for a summer table decoration. I used a mixture of artificial and dried flowers, choosing artificial raspberries, orange daisies and hydrangea florets, and dried matricaria, yellow achillea heads, clover and a few dark red helichrysums, all of which were arranged on a brown oasis cone. This was set in a low pedestal vase and then wired in place. The use of both dried and artificial flowers in an arrangement gives it a rich yet soft texture and appearance.

When making this little tree, I would suggest that you arrange the achillea, matricaria and hydrangea florets first, and only after you have inserted all of these, add the other materials. Start at the bottom of the cone and work your way around until you reach the top. You should wire the dried flowers into clumps, to give them more form and density, using silver stub wires. There is no need to wire the artificial flowers and the raspberries, however, as they are sold ready-mounted.

PINK AND PEARL TREE

This is an unusual tree for Christmas, but its pastel colours and different textures give it plenty of impact and make it a refreshing change from more classic and traditional trees. Apart from the silver baubles, of course, there is very little about this tree that is specifically Christmassy, and you might festoon it with bells and doves for a winter engagement party.

Follow the instructions for the Fruit Pyramid, as shown in the second step on page 62 and on pages 74–5, but use brown oasis instead of green. Firstly, twist pink lining material around an old sheet to make a thick rope of fabric. Alternatively, you could use a stiffened fabric, as described on page 19, or paper ribbon.

Like wired ribbon, incidentally, this last can be very difficult to obtain, though I sell it in my shops and I feel that it is so useful and decorative that hopefully a lot more outlets will sell it in the future. It comes in very tightly-bound rolls, rather like a coiled rope, and has to be untwisted before you can use it. The dyes used resemble vegetable dyes – mossy greens, tomato red, and powdery blue – so the effect is subtle rather than garish, and I use it a great deal, not only in trees but in the full range of Christmas decorations and in combination with dried flowers. It can be used to add bulk to garlands, and to make attractive decorative bows. The general effect is of crêpe paper rather than smooth – definitely something worth looking for and fun to experiment with.

Starting from the top, swirl the fabric or ribbon around the tree in a spiral and pin the ends into the oasis with 1.25mm (18 gauge) stub wires, making sure that they are absolutely secure.

Another way of achieving a spiral effect is to arrange a contrasting foliage, such as blue pine, box or any suitable sprigs of foliage from your garden, in a spiral band down the length of the tree. If you decide to do this, you must arrange the box or pine spiral before you insert any other materials, and you must make sure that you pack it very tightly, so that you create a solid, dramatic effect, setting up a contrast with the flowers.

When you have fixed the rope in position, or arranged a spiral of foliage, add the dried peonies, cutting the stems down to about 17.5cm (7in) and sticking them directly into the oasis. Arrange the marjoram and dried green foliage in clumps to prevent the arrangement looking bitty.

When you have arranged the flowers, position the baubles, using long 1.25mm (18 gauge) wire pins. Now check that neither the oasis nor the wire is visible, and fill in any holes that you find with more dried peonies.

The pot can be loosely covered with some soft pink material, lace and beads. Alternatively, you might decide to put it into a larger suitable container, but I find that something that is loose and unformed, like the drapery in the picture, is aesthetically more pleasing.

SMALL WHITE TREE

This is an ideal arrangement for a table for a wedding or late spring party, or the centrepiece for a formal dinner party. Rather than a branch, I made this from a solid cone of wet green oasis.

When making tight floral arrangements like this one, remember not to put all the flowers on the same level, but to increase their depth and texture by placing some very close to the oasis and others further out. You should also let some of the flowers gently break the symmetry of the arrangement to soften the general outline. Arrange two or three slightly longer pieces of trailing ivy at the bottom of the cone so that they droop down on the vase, thus avoiding any stark finish between the bowl and the flowers.

HYDRANGEA AND PEONY TREE

This small tree of dried flowers and a few artificial fruits is very quick to make, as all the flowers are quite large. It would, therefore, be a good arrangement to choose if you wanted to decorate a table but were rather short of time.

I used dried hydrangeas, peonies, roses, helichrysum and pine cones, all of which I wired up, together with artificial plums and berries, and a few small bows. Place a cone of brown oasis in your chosen container, then arrange the hydrangea flowers first, as they are the largest and bulkiest, followed by the peonies, roses, artificial plums, artificial berries, pine cones and helichrysum, in that order. Finally, tuck a few small wired bows into any gaps as a finishing touch.

FRUIT PYRAMID

This exotic pyramid of fruits can be made up to 1.5 metres (5 feet) tall, for a very dramatic display (any higher and it's likely to fall over), or as little as 30cm (12in) high for a table decoration. However big or small you make this arrangement, it will be easiest to work *in situ*, as it is extremely heavy when completed, and is therefore very difficult to move. Try to plan your decorations so that your pyramid will stand on the floor – it is much easier to work on the floor when making such a large pyramid, and it is also safer. The last thing you want is your pyramid toppling over and crashing to the floor as guests move around a buffet table!

Choose a very straight branch that is at least 5cm (2in) thick if you are making a large pyramid, as it will then support and balance the finished arrangement. Set the branch in plaster in the normal way. The base structure is made in the same way as for the tree described on page 62, but if you are making a large pyramid you will need to use six blocks of wet green oasis, wrapping these securely in wire netting.

Hammer three strong nails vertically into the top of the branch, then hammer another three 30cm (12in) below them, and a further three 30cm (12in) below the second three. Place an oasis block lengthways to the branch and secure it to one of the topmost nails with a 1.25mm (18 gauge) wire, then fix the bottom of the block to the next row of nails. Repeat this to secure two more blocks to the top of the branch, then firmly attach the other three oasis blocks in the same way to the second and third rows of nails.

Once you are sure that all the oasis blocks are secure, pin all the fruits and/or vegetables on to the pyramid, using 1.25mm (18 gauge) stub wires. You can use either all fruits, or all vegetables, or a mixture of the two. A few flowers, and definitely a certain quantity of foliage, will help to lighten the effect and can be used to fill in any gaps.

For this pyramid, I used bananas, pineapples, black and green grapes, green apples, peaches, oranges and chestnut mushrooms. This will give you a good variety of shapes and textures, so that cutting the fruit in halves or quarters will be unnecessary, which means that your pyramid will last longer. When you have added all the fruits, fill in any gaps with foliages.

To decorate the container, wrap a doubled length of wire netting around it, securing the ends of the netting together with 1.25mm (18 gauge) stub wires. Cut 25cm (10in) lengths of boxwood and weave these through the netting. Keep weaving stems through the netting until all the netting is obscured and you have created a hedge effect.

Box hedging can be used in a variety of ways, either to line two sides of a walkway, or even to cover walls. It is a very useful way of obscuring such unsightly things as water tanks, pipes, or compost boxes, to beautify your garden or patio for a party. Outside, box hedging should last for at least a week in normal conditions, if it is sprayed regularly. Indoors, it will dry, but it can still look effective if you spray it with a dark green spray paint.

BALL TREES

Like cone trees, ball trees have the advantage of taking up comparatively little space, yet they can still make a dramatic impact. At their worst, they can be dreary, dusty arrangements on straight sticks, of the type that would do little to embellish any home, but if the basic construction is used with a sense of style and imagination they can be fun, and a definite asset.

One of the most essential things is to begin by selecting the container and the branch. The former should be attractive and appropriate to the area in which the finished decoration will be placed. The branch that is being used to make the trunk will be fixed in plaster, so if your container is valuable you will have to use a removable inner container, such as a plastic flower pot. The branch must be in keeping with the flowers – definitely not a length of bamboo or a broom handle, but something with a bit of character and texture. For example, if you are making a ball tree for a heavy fireplace, then I suggest a short, thick stem, whereas a trunk for a tree that is to be placed on a dressing table should be slender and delicate, but should still have character. Sometimes it can look attractive if you entwine two or more stems, perhaps of ivy or honeysuckle, instead of using a single branch to make the trunk.

Most ball trees are made with dried or artificial material, but fresh flowers or greenery can be used for a special occasion. They are a little time-consuming, and extravagant because they do not last very long, but they make a good talking point.

A little tree, like this gypsophila ball (see page 79), makes a perfect decoration for a bedside or dressing table, and a fresh flower tree of this type can also be a pretty table arrangement for a wedding or a summer party, giving a light, delicate effect. If you look closely, you will notice that most of the gypsophila is fully in flower – the perfect stage at which to use it.

Ball trees

Set a branch into nylon reinforced plaster (see page 62). Take an oasis ball and, using a knife, cut a small hole for the branch. Push the oasis ball on to the top of the branch and then cover the ball with wire netting. Secure the netting on to itself. If you wish to make a fresh ball tree, use blocks of soaked green oasis – quarter, half or whole size – setting three around the top of the tree. These must be secured to a nail set in the top of the trunk (see page 62).

If you feel that you need added security, you can hammer nails to the trunk below the oasis, and wire the netting to these. Otherwise, you can simply wire the netting to the trunk of the tree. Make sure that the netting is pressed as closely around the ball as possible. An alternative method of securing an oasis ball to a pole is to use a hot glue gun, if you have one, but this is not as secure as the first method.

Making a moss ball

To make a moss ball, I suggest that you use bung moss, which is a dark green moss with a smooth surface. Before using the moss, turn the pieces upside down and cut out the roots – when you look at the underside of the moss, there will be a black area, a light brown one, and finally the green top. Using a pair of scissors, cut off the black area. This will give a smooth finish to your ball and will ensure that the pieces fit closely together.

Don't be tempted to use pieces of moss larger than 7.5cm (3in) across; if you do this, you will find that the pieces crack apart when you position them on the ball. In any case, you will find that smaller pieces are easier to handle and to jigsaw together. To keep each piece of moss in place, use a 10cm (4in) length of 1.25mm (18 gauge) stub wire, bent in half to form a pin. Push this through the moss and into the oasis, pushing it sufficiently far in to conceal the top of the wire. If you have a glue gun, you can glue the moss to the oasis, and you will find that this is the most successful way of making this type of tree.

A gypsophila tree

To make a gypsophila tree, gather a generous bunch of flower heads in your hand, then wire them as shown on page 26. Trim the wire so that it extends only approximately 7.5cm (3in) below the stems. Use the same type of wiring to make similar bunches of other flowers and foliage, such as lavender, edelweiss or shamrock. These trees look delightful, but you will find that to achieve a good coverage you will need a surprisingly large quantity of flowers.

Always start by placing the first bunch of flowers at the top of the ball, and insert succeeding bunches closely together, so that you avoid ending up with bald patches. You may notice that I used fresh flowers in dry oasis for this gypsophila ball, but the dry variety of gypsophila is not so easily wired and does not give such a dense coverage as the fresh flowers. As the fresh bunches gradually dry out, they will keep their shape and colour and will continue to give good coverage.

LICHEN TREE
WITH GLASS BAUBLES

Not everyone likes very pretty Christmas trees, in which case this sophisticated tree might appeal instead.

Find a straight branch, then set one end into a pot filled with plaster. Once the plaster has set firm, push the top of the branch into a ball of brown oasis, and cover the oasis with lichen moss and wire netting, securing it to the branch with 0.71mm (22 gauge) stub wires. Choose some contorted lichen-covered branches, such as hawthorn twigs, and trim about 10cm (4in) from the bottom of each stem to make it easier to push them into the oasis. Then add stems of blue pine, stripped of their lower needles. In the spaces between the lichen twigs and the blue pine, place clumps of lichen moss, then add a few glass baubles.

The finished result should be spiky and with a good mixture of blue pine, lichen twigs and lichen moss.

MOSS TREE

This little tree relies on its texture and shape for its success, so try to choose the nicest bung moss and most interesting branch you can! Once you have done so, push one end of the branch into a pot of plaster and leave until set. Then place this inside a decorative basket. Cover the top of the plaster with bung moss.

You will notice that this trunk is actually composed of more than one branch twisted together, in which case you cannot just push the oasis ball on to the top of the branch. Instead, press the ball of brown oasis on to the top of the branch until it leaves little indentations, then cut these out to a depth of 2.5cm (1in) and a width slightly narrower than the branches themselves. Squeeze a little glue into the holes, then push the ball on to the branches and leave until the glue has set. Arrange the moss as shown on page 79.

PROTEA TREE

When making a flower ball tree it must have a strong sharp shape for maximum impact, and this exotic combination of two types of protea, miniature ornamental pineapple tops, pale pink roses, hyacinths and 'Cheer' narcissi achieves that perfectly. I used the pineapple tops as the inspiration for the arrangement, choosing my colours from their pinks and creams.

Set a branch in a pot of nylon reinforced plaster and leave to dry, then push a ball of wet green oasis, wrapped in wire netting, on to the top of the branch and wire in place. You can then arrange the flowers. I then put the pot into a dark basket, as a light-coloured container would have made the flowers look top-heavy. To hide the surface of the plaster, I covered it with clumps of bung moss, wired into place.

If you don't have a suitably coloured basket you could always spray one, using either florists' or car paint spray, but do remember to do this outdoors, preferably, or in a well-ventilated room, as the fumes are highly toxic and can build up, becoming extremely strong.

WINTER TREE

This would make an unusual Christmas decoration, but in fact it is wintery rather than Christmassy, and would look most effective on a mantelpiece.

Fresh blue pine has been used, but this will dry out in time, and the tree could happily last all year round, if you wanted to keep it. Apart from the pine, all the other ingredients – dried fungi, pine cones, nuts, lichen moss and artificial fruit – will last indefinitely. All you need do is to dust it from time to time with a hair drier.

As the fresh pine is intended to dry out, I used a brown oasis ball. You could, of course, use the green variety without soaking it, but this would tend to crumble and would not hold the materials as well. It is advisable to set your trunk in a plastic pot which can be placed inside a more attractive cache pot.

EDELWEISS AND POPPY HEAD TREE

When making a tree as small as this it is important to get the little details correct. For example, the basic colours of the dried edelweiss and poppy heads are grey and light brown, so the branch on which they are set should ideally have the same sort of colouring.

Once you have found a suitable branch, make the tree in the usual way, using a ball of brown oasis, covered in wire netting, held in place with wires. When decorating the oasis ball, you will find that the stems of the poppy heads are strong enough to be inserted into the oasis without being wired first, but the edelweiss, which are more fragile, will need to be wired. As they are too small on their own, it is best to wire the edelweiss flowers in groups of three, which will both save time and give density to the finished arrangement.

LAVENDER TREE

What could be better than to have a decorative small tree that is also scented? This lavender tree smells wonderful and also looks very attractive. If you are going to make a tree for permanent display, it is best to choose only one type of flower as this is easier on the eye.

It takes a long time to make a lavender tree and you will require a sizeable quantity of flower heads to create a full appearance, because the flowers themselves are so thin. Wire them, using half-lengths of 0.71mm (22 gauge) stub wires, in clumps of ten stems that should be not more than 5–7.5cm (2–3in) long.

Form the outer circle of the flowers first, pushing the wired stems into the ball of brown oasis that you have pushed on to the top of a branch set in a container of nylon reinforced plaster, then work into the centre, keeping the bunches very close together to give a complete carpet effect.

SMALL YELLOW TREE

Fresh miniature trees, such as this one, make good decorations for dinner tables, buffet arrangements, side tables or anywhere else that will display them to their best advantage.

I chose a basket for this tree, and therefore had to line it with black plastic before filling it with plaster and inserting the branch for the trunk. The plaster is quite thick, but even so it will inevitably ooze through the gaps of an unlined basket. As this is a fresh flower tree, soaked green oasis was used. When you are making a fresh arrangement of this type, you should position the foliages first, followed by the flowers in order of size, working from the largest down to the smallest.

For this tree, I used a combination of white phlox, white freesias and yellow moss roses.

AUTUMN TREE

This tree uses a mixture of artificial flowers and foliage – viburnum, hydrangeas, red roses and seeded grasses – and a few artificial fruits, the colours of which give an added richness to the whole arrangement. However, they would have lost their magic if the cream shades of the viburnum flowers had not been introduced, as they lighten the entire effect and thereby bring the tree to life.

It is essential to consider the textures as well as the colours when choosing artificial flowers – fortunately, there is an enormous range from which to make your selection and it is worth spending a little extra to buy top quality flowers with subtle colours. If you keep the arrangement free from dust – the occasional blow with a hair drier on a low setting will help – and out of harsh sunlight, it should last a long time.

PINE CONE TREE

With the exception of the nuts, all the basic ingredients of this tree could be collected on a woodland walk, or even from your own garden, if you grow suitable trees! For extra interest, make sure that you choose cones of varying sizes.

The finished tree has a wonderful texture, combined with beautifully subtle colours that make it perfect for a Harvest or Christmas arrangement, and I think that it is best placed at eye level, so that the varying shapes of the cones can be examined at leisure. If you wish to put your tree into a garlanded basket, as I have done here, it is best to make the garland around the basket first (see page 26). After this, line the basket with plastic, and set the trunk in plaster in the normal way. Wire the large cones individually, using 1.25mm (18 gauge) stub wires, but group the smaller ones in clumps of five and seven, using 0.71mm (22 gauge) wires.

SHAMROCK TREE

If you make a tree with shamrocks, they will only last for 24 hours, but then so does St Patrick's Day.

Choose a suitable branch and set it in a small plastic pot of nylon reinforced plaster. Once it has set hard, remove the branch with its plaster base from the pot, breaking this if necessary, and place the plaster base in a small glass vase. Choose a vase that is slightly larger all around than the original pot, so that you can push lichen moss between the glass and the plaster.

Cover the surface of the plaster with bung moss. The shamrocks should be wired in tiny clumps and set into green oasis. I like to leave spaces between the clumps and fill them with clumps of sphagnum moss, for added interest and texture.

PINK TREE

When making flower trees of this type, it is not necessary to use just a single main branch. Instead, as shown in this photograph, you can incorporate two- or three-stemmed branches to add more interest and give a sculptured look to the design.

If you decide to use separate branches, however, you must secure them into their final positions with 1.25mm (18 gauge) wires, and then push them into nylon reinforced plaster, otherwise they will swivel or move about. Sometimes the branches will tend to move around and slip until the plaster has set, so you may have to work out a way of propping them up until they are fixed in the plaster (it doesn't take long, so I often just stand and hold the branches for a few minutes); the nylon reinforced variety takes longer to dry than ordinary plaster, but it is much stiffer, so the problem does not usually arise when you are only using small stems like this.

You should also make sure that you leave enough space between the ends of the branches for the flowers. Here, I used deep pink ranunculus, red and pink roses, muscari, variegated ivy and eucalyptus.

Once the plaster has set, add a covering layer of bung moss to the pot. If you have used separate branches, you can either hide the joins with bung moss, or place a small piece of wet oasis – about a 5cm (2in) cube – on top of the plaster; create a small flower arrangement, and then cover both the oasis and any plaster that remains visible with moss.

Wrap two quarter-blocks of soaked green oasis in netting, then push them onto the branch ends and secure them with 1.25mm (18 gauge) stub wires.

As the ranunculuses have rather heavy heads, and the muscari stems are fairly weak, it is best to wire the stems with 0.71mm (22 gauge) stub wires. To do this, place a wire along each stem and hold it in position with thin silver wire, one end of which is pushed through the top of the flower and the other twined around them and the 0.71mm (22 gauge) wire.

I started by arranging all the roses, because they had the largest flower heads, then came the muscari, then the ranunculus. The trails of variegated ivy were used to soften the outline.

MISTLETOE BALL

Everyone knows about the Christmas tradition of kissing under the mistletoe. In fact, of course, mistletoe is not strictly a Christmas tradition, but a much older one, going back to the days of the druids. Mistletoe held great importance in the old Celtic religion as a symbol of fertility. It probably played a part in their winter solstice celebrations – held at much the same time as Christmas – where it symbolized hopes for a fertile and prosperous New Year.

Although we know very little about what actually happened in the druidic rites, couples presumably kissed under the mistletoe if they wanted children – so perhaps a mistletoe ball would be a more appropriate decoration for a winter engagement party or wedding!

Unfortunately, the Christmas mistletoe is often bought in a last-minute rush, and there are only a few sad sprigs to offer a far-from-fertile and plain unfestive invitation. But even if you do your shopping in good time, mistletoe can sometimes be hard to obtain, in which case this ball is the answer, since it is made from the plastic variety. Although artificial mistletoe may not instantly appeal to you, it has several advantages over the fresh type. For one thing, it is comparatively light in weight, and a ball made from artificial mistletoe will therefore present less of a hazard when suspended by a ribbon from the ceiling, but it also means that any berries that fall off will not make the sticky mess caused by the real

thing. What is more, the dry form of oasis can be used, so your romantic guests won't be put off by water dropping from above!

Fold a 1.25mm (18 gauge) wire into the shape of a hairpin, then push the two open ends through to the other side of a ball of brown oasis, leaving a loop some 5cm (2in) long on the top. Holding on to this loop, bend the two protruding wires away from each other and back on to the oasis ball. This keeps the oasis secure and the resulting wire loop gives you something through which the ribbon can be tied. Pass one end of a length of ribbon through the wire loop and suspend it from the ceiling, curtain rail, beam, or whatever else you have in mind.

If you decide to opt for fresh mistletoe, remember to use soaked green oasis, wrapped in wire netting, instead of the brown version. It is also best to create the arrangement in a place where the water can drain out of the oasis without causing a mess. If you have to make it *in situ*, then put down a plastic sheet covered with a dust sheet, which will catch the excess water and any of the mistletoe berries that drop in the process.

Incidentally, if you have a garden with suitable trees – an old apple tree would be ideal – you might keep a few of those berries and try to grow some mistletoe for yourself. It is a very hit-and-miss affair, but if you crush a few berries in the crook of an old branch, you might be lucky.

FESTIVE TABLES

If you enjoy flower arranging, the dinner table is one of the most important places to make dramatic arrangements. Your efforts will be seen by a captive audience, but at the same time your guests will have a good chance to examine the design closely, so you must double check that none of your mechanics are showing. This is the perfect opportunity to use a few of the more unusual materials, such as snowdrops, eucalyptus seedheads, exotic small fruits and nuts, because they will create a talking point and will attract far more notice at the centre of a dinner table than on a side table.

At the same time you must bear in mind that the flowers are there to complement the food and create a pleasant ambience, not to overpower the guests. Try not to use very heavily scented flowers, for example, and do not make an arrangement so large that guests are unable to communicate across the table. It is a good idea to place the arrangement at the centre of the table and sit on one of the chairs in order to check that the design is a good height. You might even arrange it *in situ*, but if so, you will need to be very tidy, which I personally find inhibiting.

This is a wonderful arrangement for a side table, or even the centre of the Christmas table, but remember that it is very tall, and can have an overall height of up to 1.3 metres (4 feet). Instead of using a candlestick, I placed a church candle in an Italian lily vase to add elegance and a touch of the unusual to this design. Three half-blocks of oasis were wrapped individually in wire netting and wired to the base of the candle with 0.71mm (22 gauge) stub wires. It is important to ensure that these are very securely fixed – add more stub wires, if necessary. Artificial pine, holly and mistletoe were inserted, then wired walnuts were added in clumps of three or five. The gaps were filled with wired pine cones and red artificial apples, and a few bows were added to finish the arrangement. To soften the effect, coloured ribbons might be draped downwards from the oasis blocks.

Decorating candlesticks

This is the most effective way of putting flowers around the base of the candle. Start by cutting a circle or square of black plastic, making it larger than the top of the candlestick. In the centre of the plastic, cut a hole large enough for the candle. Slip this over the candle and down on to the top of the candlestick. Position small pieces of wet oasis between the candle and the edge of the candlestick. Once they are in place, cut away any excess black plastic and trim the oasis, where necessary, for a good fit.

Cut a circular piece of wire netting, about the approximate size of the top of the candlestick, and slip this over the candle. Fold the sharp ends of the netting into the oasis, then use silver reel wire to attach the netting firmly to the candlestick. The tying wires should be as close to the top of the candlestick as possible, so that they will be concealed by the flowers and foliage. You can secure the oasis to the candle with oasis tape, but this method is very insecure and it is not advisable to do this.

On small candlesticks, it is possible to use candle cups. These are ready-made plastic containers, which fit into the candlestick. They are available in white, black, silver and gold. Either use a cylinder of oasis or cut a quarter block to the correct shape. Place your candle holder into the centre of the oasis, then tape the oasis into position, as shown in the picture. Sometimes, the bottom of the candle cup is too small or thin for the candlestick. If this is the case, either wrap some oasis tape around the cup or use a small piece of mastic to hold it in place.

Rounded arrangements

To make a mound of oasis for a high, rounded arrangement, place five blocks of oasis into a plastic tray, about 30cm (12in) in diameter, as shown. Trim the oasis into a smooth mound by cutting the corners. The resulting shape is suitable for an arrangement 20–25cm (8–10in) high. If you wish to make a more conical shape, add a half block of oasis to the top.

When you have a smooth, satisfactory mound of oasis, you will need to tape the pieces securely together. Use green oasis tape and take it over the mound and under the tray. You will need to use two lengths of tape, crossing them underneath the tray. Remember, when making a table arrangement, that it will be seen by seated guests, so the lower portion will be visible. When you are making the arrangement, it is therefore important to ensure that the base is well covered.

Oval arrangements

For a long, thin or oval table arrangement, place one block of soaked oasis on an oasis tray. Trim the corners with a knife, and then tape the block in place. Start by placing longer pieces of foliage at either end, and then place shorter lengths down the sides. If the oasis projects above the level of the container, as is the case, for example, with an oasis tray, you must remember to water the arrangement at least twice a day, or the oasis will very rapidly dry out.

HOLLY AND NUTS
TABLE DECORATION

I think that well-dressed tables are one of the principal pleasures of Christmas, as they enhance the warm feeling that this season traditionally has. I like the simple, elegant mixture of blue pine, holly, walnuts and pine cones in this table decoration, and find it quite refreshing and a restful change from all the glitter, gold and silver that Christmas usually seems to bring.

To make it, soak a block of green oasis in water until it is thoroughly wet, then place it on a black oasis tray. Insert two candle holders into the top of the oasis, then tape the block of oasis to the black tray, as though it were a parcel, using green oasis tape. Put the candles into their holders, but do not remove their plastic wrappings yet as these will help to protect the candles from any damage while the arrangement is being made.

Take the tips of blue pine and strip the needles from the lower part of each small branch. Cover the top and sides of the oasis block in blue pine until all the oasis is hidden. Then add the holly, having first stripped it of its lower leaves. Follow this by adding the wired pine cones and then the wired nuts. This oval shape is a good alternative to a round advent table arrangement and will be the best choice if your table is rectangular.

CAROUSEL
ADVENT RING

Like the Holly and Nuts arrangement, this advent ring is also constructed on soaked green oasis, in this case a ring. Once the candle holders and then the lengths of pine have been positioned, cut three 25cm (10in) lengths of uncoiled paper ribbon. Taking each length in turn, attach a 0.71mm (22 gauge) stub wire to each end of the ribbon, winding the wire around the end several times to hold it tightly. Trim the wires so that there is a length of about 5cm (2in) of wire at each end of the ribbons, and insert these wires into the oasis to hold the ribbon strips in place.

When the lengths of ribbon are evenly distributed around the ring, add the carousel horses. The cherubs were also of frosted plastic, and artificial plums and pine cones completed the ring.

You will have to be careful when watering this ring, or the paper ribbon will be damaged, as will the artificial fruit.

FLORAL CANDLESTICK

With a candlestick of this size, to use anything but large flowers in the arrangement would have created an unbalanced effect. The lavish blend of flowers and foliages used here – 'La Rêve' lilies, 'Lovely Girl' roses, soft pink roses, catkins, kangaroo paws and eucalyptus – makes a stunning decoration for a midsummer party, especially one with romantic overtones, such as an engagement party or perhaps a dinner to celebrate a wedding anniversary.

If you decorate a large candlestick of this type, you will not be able to use a candlecup, so you will have to make your own support, using black plastic, wire netting and wires, as shown on page 96. Don't let this deter you from making the effort – the results will be worth the trouble and the technique is not difficult to master. Take care when making the arrangement to allow sufficient downward trailing foliage to conceal the mechanics.

FLOWER, FRUIT AND CANDLE ARRANGEMENT

A green oasis advent ring has here been used for an arrangement that would be ideal for a Harvest supper or a Thanksgiving dinner. The nectarines, which are wired with 1.25mm (18 gauge) stub wires, are very heavy, and will fall out of the oasis ring if it is moved, so it is best to make this arrangement *in situ*. If this is not possible, I suggest that you remove the nectarines before moving the arrangement and replace them once it is in its new position. This will also make it easier to arrange the flowers to sit flush with the table, hiding the oasis ring and base, which can all too easily be left visible to seated guests.

MISTLETOE TABLE

To make a long, dramatic table arrangement of this type, I suggest that you use a tray of the kind made to fit under a window box to catch the drips. Fill the tray, which should be 1 metre (3 feet) long, with blocks of brown oasis, if you are intending to use artificial mistletoe. Use soaked green oasis if your mistletoe is fresh. Cover the blocks with a sheet of wire netting and secure this to the tray with silver reel wire. If the arrangement is to be placed on a polished wooden surface, you will have to remember to put a mat underneath to avoid scratches.

Next, insert the candle holders, followed by the candles. As usual, leave these in their plastic wrappers to protect them from damage while the arrangement is being created. It is helpful to make the decoration with the candles in place as they will give you an idea of the general height and appearance of the finished arrangement.

When the candles are in place, add clumps of artificial mistletoe and pine, and large clear glass baubles, securing them with 1.25mm (18 gauge) stub wires.

Although fresh mistletoe is very lovely, it is preferable to use artificial mistletoe for an arrangement such as this one, because the fresh berries are juicy and drop very quickly, staining the surface on which the decoration is placed.

HOLLY ADVENT RING

Advent rings don't have to be made solely for adults – they can be perfect for children too, as this one shows, and if you use holly, as I have done in this case, this will deter them from pulling the arrangement apart.

Soak a ring of green oasis in water, then insert the four candle holders, followed by the candles, still wrapped in their protective plastic sleeves.

When the candles are in position, cover the oasis completely with sprigs of holly, stripped of their lower leaves. Here, I wired up and then added a few Christmas decorations to the arrangement, before removing the plastic candle wrappings.

However hard you try to avoid spoiling candles, they will sometimes look a bit smeary and smudged by the time they are in position – perhaps because they have been lying in a box since last year. To make them look as good as new, get an old bucket and boil a kettle of water. Leave the

water to stand for about five minutes so that it is not absolutely scalding. Holding the candle by the wick so that it hangs over the bucket – you can use a pair of long-nosed pliers as a safety measure – pour the hot water over the candle, turning it slowly around. Just a little water should be all that is needed to restore the smooth surface, and the water should be poured on in a quick gush to flow rapidly all down the length of the candle. If you take too long, you will end up with a bubbly, streaked candle. Use a bucket; if you use the kitchen sink it may well get blocked with wax.

Make sure that the decorations aren't placed too close to the candles or they may catch fire. You might choose decorations similar to those on your Christmas tree, in order to create a feeling of continuity. As an alternative, you could use variegated holly with berries, and this is a combination that I feel is at its most beautiful when left unadorned.

If all the fresh advent rings and table decorations described in this book are to look their best, they will need some after-care. At the end of each evening, it is a very good idea, therefore, to take the arrangement off the table and place it on the draining board, where you should water it very carefully, using a small watering can. Use enough water to moisten the oasis, without ruining the decorations. This will considerably prolong the life of the arrangement, and will help it to last two or three times longer than it would do if left unwatered.

GOLDEN ADVENT RING

This is a rich, luscious decoration for a side table or the centre of a dining table, using blue pine, pine cones, walnuts, chestnuts, artificial gold grapes, golden cherubs and brown bows. To achieve the slightly glittered effect on the cones, spray them with adhesive, then lightly sprinkle them with just a small quantity of gold glitter and allow them to dry.

Soak a green oasis ring in water; space the four candle holders evenly around the circle and then add the cherubs. These are wired from the back, using 1.25mm (18 gauge) stub wires. Alternatively, you could tape toothpicks (wooden cocktail sticks) to their legs, which will hold them just as securely as the wire.

Cover the ring completely with blue pine tips that have been stripped of their bottom needles, then add the candles in their plastic wrappings. Next, arrange the wired grapes, cones, nuts and finally the bows, before removing the plastic wrappings from the candles.

APPLES AND NIGHTLIGHTS

A table decoration like this is a wonderful way in which to welcome guests on a cold winter's night, and the little glowing flames are almost guaranteed to make them feel warmer. If you feel that it is too large an arrangement for the dining table, you could place it on a side table, or perhaps in a hallway.

To create it, you will need plenty of blue pine, at least twenty red apples and ten nightlights. Pile soaked green oasis into a large low flat dish, then carve it into a mound with a sharp kitchen knife. Cover with wire netting, securing it to the dish with silver reel wire. Strip the lower needles from twigs of blue pine, about 15cm (6in) long, then arrange them in the mound of oasis until this has been completely covered.

Taking about ten of the apples, and a sharp, thin-bladed knife, carve a hole in the top of each one, big enough to take a nightlight. Place a nightlight, unlit, into each hole, then arrange all the apples, with and without nightlights, in the oasis, using 1.25mm (18 gauge) stub wires to hold them in place. Light the nightlights at least half an hour before the guests are due to arrive, as they will burn better, but do watch to make sure that you haven't left any blue pine hanging over the candle flames, as this could become a serious fire hazard.

TARTAN TABLE DESIGN

Used to cover the table at Christmas time, a tartan cloth gives a very festive feeling to any occasion and is also practical for a party, as it does not show as many stains as a plain cloth would. This arrangement uses blue pine, pine cones, artificial fruit, fresh red apples and tartan bows, which are made from ribbon, as shown on page 12.

Soak a block of green oasis in water until it is wet, then place it on a black oasis tray. Insert the two candle holders and tape the oasis in position, using green oasis tape. Add the candles – as usual, these should be in their plastic wrappings, to prevent them being damaged. Cover all the oasis with tips of blue pine, from which all the lower needles have been stripped.

Next, add the red apples to give a heavy, rich feeling to the arrangement, pinning them to the oasis with 1.25mm (18 gauge) stub wires. Vary the way in which you wire the apples, pushing some of the stub wires through from top to bottom and others from side to side.

When you have positioned the fresh apples, arrange the artificial fruit, which is already wired, and then the cones, which should be wired on 0.71mm (22 gauge) stub wires. Finally, position the tartan bows and remove the candle wrappings.

ARRANGEMENTS

This is probably the most traditional and for general purposes perhaps the most practical section of this book. Although the decorations in this book are intended primarily for festive occasions, a lot of the arrangements shown here are made with dried materials and would outlast any special occasion.

The best time to buy dried flowers, especially flowers such as peonies, marjoram and larkspur, is from September through to January, because the spring and summer flowers have dried out and are ready for sale by September, so this is when all the new stock reaches the shops. By the end of January many of the standard dried flowers are in short supply, though a lot of the Australian and more exotic dried materials are still available.

Such a wide range of fresh flowers is now available that it is impossible even to start to cover the possibilities, but we have tried to give some ideas for interesting mixtures of colour, texture and shape, which is the secret of success in all arrangements. Remember that lavish-looking arrangements, like the one shown here, can often be more economical than you might suppose, incorporating a mixture of garden and hedgerow flowers and foliage with just a small selection of expensive items.

This mixture of pink cherry blossom, lilies, cow parsley, eucalyptus, white blossom, lilac and pink nerines is one of my favourites. The pink blossom and lilac give strength to the arrangement, and their heavy round shapes contrast well with the sharp outlines of the nerines. The cow parsley was chosen for its foam-like flowers, and I used eucalyptus to cool down the warm pink tones. Fill your chosen vase with water, then push down some crumpled wire netting into the top. Don't use too much netting, or you will find that it is difficult to insert the thick stems of lilac and blossom. The nerines should be left until the last, because they will stand out and need to be placed for maximum effect.

Dried flower arrangements

It is advisable to wire most dried flowers, as the stems tend to be rather weak. Only a few, such as poppy seedheads or carthamus flowers, can be left on their stems and used without wiring, as their stems are so strong. Roses can be used on their own or clumped together. If you wish to make dried flowers longer, then mount them on green sticks, using stub wires to hold them in place. To wire flowers, use the same method as shown on page 26.

If you are making a dried flower arrangement in a basket, choose one with an appropriate texture and shape for the flowers that you will be using. There is such a wide range available that it is worth taking the trouble to look around. Place brown oasis in the bottom of the basket and cover it with sphagnum moss. After this, lay a piece of wire netting over the moss and secure it to the basket by pushing a stub wire through both the netting and the basket and then twisting it on itself. Do this at four evenly-spaced points around the basket.

When placing dried flowers into the basket, place all the flowers of one type – carthamus, for example – in position, keeping them clumped in evenly-distributed groups. Move on to the next type only when you have inserted all the flowers of the first variety. You will find that you must clump flowers of the same type and colour so that they show up, and give a luxurious feel to the arrangement – if they are too thinly scattered, their effect is diminished, and the entire arrangement will tend to look bitty and unsatisfying.

Arranging fresh flowers

I generally recommend wire netting to hold fresh flowers, as they tend to last longer this way. On the other hand, oasis, provided it lies below the level of the container, will retain moisture longer without a topping up. Wire netting comes in two different gauges – 2.5cm (1in) and 5cm (2in). I find that the 5cm (2in) size is more versatile, as the holes of the smaller size are often too small for the stems, once the netting has been crumpled. Start rolling the netting at one corner and tuck the ends in as you work. Make sure that the finished roll is not too tight for the flowers.

When you have placed the netting in the bowl, it should protrude at least 5cm (2in) above the rim; this will give extra stability to the longer stems. For a small arrangement, use silver reel wire or oasis tape to attach the wire netting to the container. For a larger arrangement, use black reel wire. Silver reel wire or plastic-coated wire is the best type to use for containers that are valuable, as the black reel wire tends to rust. When your flowers have finished, always cut the netting out of the bowl; leave it to dry, and wash out the container, otherwise the wire netting will rust and will mark your bowl.

If you are going to be travelling with your arrangement, or it is intended for someone who will not remember to water it – if, for example, it is going to a hospital or a hotel – then oasis is your best bet, as you can empty out the water while you transport the arrangement, and refill it when you reach your destination. If you used wire netting, the stems would dry out in transit. Some flowers, such as carnations, chrysanthemums or lilies, do not particularly mind being in oasis, whereas roses, mimosa and genista will suffer.

FRESH FLORAL ARRANGEMENT

This is another of my favourite mixtures of colours: pinky creams, blues, yellows and whites. I used 'Casablanca' lilies, 'Porcelain' roses, blue bee, *Euphorbia marginata*, eucalyptus and rape. The lilies are for contrast, giving freshness, strength and weight to the other flowers, all of which are small-headed.

Choose a container that will fit inside a larger basket, then place some crumpled wire netting in the container and tape it in place with green oasis tape or wire it securely with silver reel wire, then fill the container with water. When using euphorbia it is important to condition it first, by leaving the stems in boiling water for at least 20 minutes before arranging them. Position the eucalyptus and euphorbia first, to give the basic shape, then add the rape, lilies, blue bee and finally the roses.

BLUE AND BURGUNDY BASKET

Arrangements of dried flowers can last for anything up to a year if they are kept out of bright sunlight and damp atmospheres, which can quickly lead to mildew. To arrange dried flowers, always use brown oasis, which is destined to be used dry and is intended solely for use with dried and artificial flowers.

A wide and interesting range of dried flowers is now available at many different outlets, including the larger garden centres and department stores as well as specialist shops, giving great scope for interesting designs. Very often, however, dried flower arrangements can look rather musty and past their best almost from the beginning, so it pays to look around and search for top quality materials.

The first thing is to check out the shop itself and make sure that you only buy from somewhere that has a rapid turnover. Dried flowers fade in the sun, so they should be kept out of direct sunlight, and they should have a good natural colour.

Dried flowers are also fragile and easily broken, so the bunches should not be crushed tightly together or some of the stems will be broken. When you inspect them carefully, gently folding back the wrapping around an individual bunch, if necessary, you will be able to see if there are headless or broken stems. As dried flowers are so prone to mould, you should also look to see if you can detect any little black spots or signs of mildew.

If the flowers or seedheads have been gathered too late in the season, they will disintegrate very rapidly; a gentle shake will reveal whether there are likely to be problems of this nature. At the same time, you should check seedheads and bulrushes for cracks and splits.

Dried flowers in prime condition are inevitably expensive, but well worth the extra money, and you can always economize to some extent by mixing cheaper flowers in with more expensive and exotic flowers and seeds, as has been done in this arrangement, where the cheaper helichrysum to some extent offsets the cost of the more expensive flowers such as the roses.

When choosing dried materials, it is very important to consider the texture of each piece as well as its colour and shape. In this arrangement, containing bunnies' ears, dried roses, pale pink helichrysum, artificial plums, lavender, delphiniums and dried thistles, I used the dark artificial plums to give depth and a lusciousness to the dried flowers, and also to pull the delphiniums into the arrangement.

HARVEST ARRANGEMENT

The colours and shapes of this arrangement remind me of a hedgerow in the autumn. To make it, I used peach artificial fruits, dried bunnies' ears, red roses, button daisies, dill and green amaranthus. The bunnies' ears were chosen because they soften the overall outline and help to give a natural flow to the dried arrangement.

I grouped the white daisies in clumps to balance the heaviness of the artificial fruits. Artificial fruits add a new dimension to dried flower arrangements, giving them weight and an added richness. When using artificial fruits you will find that it is preferable to take them off their original stem and wire them individually.

The amaranthus was selected for its sharp shape and the dill was used to soften the arrangement and fill the intervening spaces with delicacy. The red roses echo the shades of the artificial fruits, to tie the arrangement together and give it cohesion.

WINTER VELVET

When using dried hydrangeas, I recommend positioning them first, as they take up a great deal of space and therefore dominate the final arrangement. Here, I also used dried red roses, red helichrysum, peachy-pink roses, marjoram and green ambrosinia. The helichrysum was placed in groups to balance the visual weight of the hydrangeas, and the peach roses were used in smaller clumps to soften the strength of the hydrangeas and helichrysum.

The light feel was produced by spreading the red roses, marjoram and green ambrosinia through the arrangement, which would make an ideal Christmas gift.

LARCH
TWIGS IN
A TANK

This is an alternative Christmas decoration for a side-table. Place two blocks of wet green oasis on top of each other in a glass tank, then stuff lichen moss between the oasis and the glass until all the oasis has been hidden from view. Cover the top of the oasis with a flat piece of wire netting and tape it in four places to the glass tank with white oasis tape.

Spray some larch twigs with just a touch of artificial white snow to accentuate the shape of the branches. When you spray, hold the can close to the branch so that you have a dense coverage, looking like little drifts of snow.

When the snow has dried, which will take about five to ten minutes, arrange the branches, not too densely, in the oasis. Add the blue pine. The pieces of blue pine should be chosen carefully because if they are too heavy they will tend to flop over. You will need three or four straight lengths for the back and middle of the arrangement, and three more softly flowing pieces for the front. Next, add white 'Casablanca' lilies, from which the stamens have been removed. This will stop the pollen from marking the lily petals, and also your clothing. The lilies should be bought at least a week before you require them so that they have a chance to open.

To finish, hang silver glitter stars on the larch twigs. You could add silver baubles, but be careful not to overdecorate or you will lose the natural effect.

MIDSUMMER SPLENDOUR

Who said that dried flowers are boring? Dried flowers no longer have to be just brown or cream, for the latest techniques enable flowers to retain their original strong colours once they have been dried. As a result, dried flowers are more versatile than ever before, and offer tremendous scope to any imaginative flower arranger. Even if you usually hate them, this arrangement will make you change your mind. I love it because it reminds me of summer and looks like a painting. It contains dried pink peonies, blue larkspur, pink clover, marjoram and green ambrosinia, pushed into blocks of brown oasis, which were first placed in the basket.

Peonies are marvellous when dried, and it is easy to dry them yourself. When a fresh peony has reached perfection, pick it, then hang it upside down in an airing cupboard – or any other place that is suitably warm and dry – for a week or two, until it feels crisp to the touch and completely free from damp. If you are unsure whether the flower is quite dry, it is best to leave it for a little while longer, otherwise it could become mildewed.

When making an arrangement of this type, it is easiest if you put in the wired clumps of marjoram first, to outline your basic shape. You can then follow with ambrosinia, blue larkspur, and lastly the peonies, which will give density and a softness of colour.

YELLOW AND WHITE BASKET

Instead of always choosing a decorative vase for a fresh flower arrangement, you can strike out in a different direction, or perhaps hide an old or chipped vase, by placing it in a larger basket or wicker container, as I have done here.

The flowers used are cow parsley, guelder roses, cream lilies, 'Golden Shower' orchids, white Canterbury bells and kangaroo paw. The Canterbury bells give a clean, fresh look to the arrangement, and the yellow orchids and roses add strength and colour. I chose the guelder roses and kangeroo paw because I think that lime green sets off yellow and white perfectly. You will notice that there is no foliage in this arrangement, but I think that the guelder roses serve the same purpose admirably.

When using cow parsley, guelder roses and Canterbury bells, you must first condition them by leaving the stems in about 5cm (2in) of boiling water for at least 10 minutes, and then leaving them in cold water for 24 hours, if possible. This will prolong their lives and make them last two or three times longer than they would without this treatment.

Hold the flowers in place by using some crumpled wire netting in the top of the vase. Oasis is not suitable as it will not allow the cow parsley, roses and Canterbury bells – all of which prefer to be directly in water – to drink, and they would soon fade.

WINTER BASKET

The cool colours of this basket arrangement are ideal for decorating rooms in the winter months, and the berried holly and starry-shaped bracts of the poinsettias make it especially suitable for Christmas, particularly if you want to avoid the traditional colours of red and green so often seen at this time of year.

I used two real stems of pine cones, and artificial frosted pine, poinsettias, mistletoe, pine with cones and holly. Fill your chosen basket with brown oasis (if you are using artificial flowers), cover with wire netting, and secure to the top of the basket with silver reel wire.

Poinsettias are available with bracts of red, white-green, pale pink, bright pink and even salmon, so there is no need at all to keep to red. You can, of course, use fresh flowers instead of the artificial ones used here, but you must then use the poinsettias as whole plants, because if you cut off the bracts they will soon fade.

If you decide to use fresh plants, line the basket with black plastic; fill it with blocks of wet green oasis, and cover with wire netting, wiring the mechanics in place. Water poinsettia plants well; leave them for about an hour, then remove them from their pots and wrap the root balls in thick plastic. Once the root ball has been securely wrapped, push two green garden sticks into the ball and use the sticks to secure the plant to the oasis, as shown on page 130. The poinsettias should then last for about five days before fading.

SANDY ARRANGEMENT

It is not often that one can use purple, yellow, peach and orange in the same arrangement, although one should never be completely governed by colour rules. If the tones and textures are pleasing, there is no reason why commonly tabooed colour combinations cannot work in an exciting and original way.

I was able to use such a mix of colours in this arrangement because the dried material – alchemilla, marjoram, yellow button chrysanthemums, peach roses and orange clover – has tones that are very muted and dusky.

The flowers were grouped together, rather than spread thinly, to give a dense, compact appearance.

BONFIRE BASKET

Just like their fresh counterparts, dried flowers can be massed in different ways to produce varied effects, and this arrangement illustrates the result of using your dried material with a very light touch. Here, I have combined dried bunnies' ears, marjoram, red roses and hydrangeas with glycerined eucalyptus. If you are tempted to experiment with dried eucalyptus you will find that the leaves fall off as you insert the stems into the arrangement (the same thing happens with dried beech). Glycerined eucalyptus is usually dyed to a darker green than the fresh leaves or to a browny pink.

The bunnies' ears and eucalyptus were chosen to soften the outline of the arrangement. The roses and marjoram were each grouped together in bunches. First, however, I wired the stems about 20cm (8in) from the top of the flower heads, so that the stems would fan out and give a more interesting and diffused appearance to the flowers.

As usual with hydrangeas, I would suggest that you position these first, so as to give depth to the arrangement. The remaining flowers can subsequently be placed so that they sit at least 7.5–10cm (3–4in) above the hydrangea heads. Since you do not need very much dried material to create this arrangement, it is very economical, and you can make two arrangements from what would usually only suffice to make one.

CONSTRUCTED TREES

Constructed trees, made by attaching flowers or small plants to bare branches, can be a very dramatic backcloth for a party and are a relatively inexpensive way of filling a large space. For example, if you are giving a party in a barn or a marquee, you might make a large, free-standing tree at the centre of the room. In this case, you must ensure that it is secure and that the branches are a good distance above the heads of the guests – you don't want to risk damage to eyes. If the party is to be held in a marquee with central poles, you can construct the trees around these. Alternatively, you might arrange trees around the walls, again making sure that the branches do not protrude dangerously into the room.

You can change the whole character of a room by creating a jungle effect, or by using a lichen tree to evoke a haunted atmosphere for a Hallowe'en party. Alternatively, you could bring the idea down to a more realistic level by creating an artificial tree to decorate a conservatory or a kitchen/dining area.

A few ideas for constructed trees are shown here, but there are numerous other possibilities. One very effective idea is to use large stems of fresh camellia, with plenty of foliage. The flowers will drop off, unfortunately, so I suggest that you buy a few artificial camellias to attach to the branches – you will find that the paler colours are the most effective.

Constructed trees, like this bare branch tree with mistletoe and candles, are fun for Christmas or New Year parties, and have a strong, architectural quality. Place the candles so that they do not lean over, and allow sufficient room between branches to ensure that the candles will not constitute a fire hazard. Here, I used artificial mistletoe, arranging it into a ball and using more to decorate the bottom of the container.

Making large trees

The setting of the branches is about the most important element in constructing a large tree, as this will govern its ultimate shape. It is also essential to make sure that the plaster is absolutely solid before you start working on the tree. The larger the tree, the larger the pot that you will need to use, and it is not a bad idea to place bricks or rocks in with the plaster, as this will add extra weight and will help to stabilize the branches as the plaster is setting.

You can extend the branches of your constructed tree by adding smaller branches, but these must be securely fastened. Overlap the branches by about 15cm (6in) and use two or three 1.25mm (18 gauge) stub wires at two or three different places to bind the two together. It is equally important that the added branches should align with the existing shape as this will help to make the join more secure. It is always better to start with a tree that is the right shape in the first place, but you may find that you have to improvise in this way.

When using plants in flower arrangements or when, as here, you are attaching them to a tree, you must remove the plant from its pot, shake off any loose soil, and wrap the root ball tightly with plant wrap. You can use any strips of thick plastic wrapping. It is important to remember to water the plant well before you wrap it, to prolong its life in the arrangement. The plastic wrapping will help to retain the moisture and it will also make the plant easier to attach to the branch or to place into an arrangement.

There should now be a tightly wrapped root ball. Push a 1.25mm (18 gauge) stub wire into the ball and take it around the ball, pushing it back into the ball where it first started. This will hold everything in position. Take a second 1.25mm (18 gauge) stub wire to attach the ball to the tree, twisting the wire securely on to itself. Always bear in mind the angle from which the tree will be seen; if people will be looking up at it, then tilt the plants forward to obscure as much of the plastic wrapping as you can, before covering the remainder with moss.

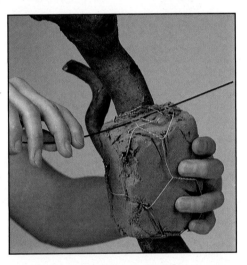

If you wish to add fresh or dried flowers to the tree, take a quarter block of the appropriate oasis and wrap it in netting. Use a 1.25mm (18 gauge) stub wire to attach it to a branch. You must attach the oasis at the top and bottom or it will swing around. Once you have positioned the flowers, check that there is no oasis visible from under, above or behind the tree. A little foliage or moss will usually be all you need.

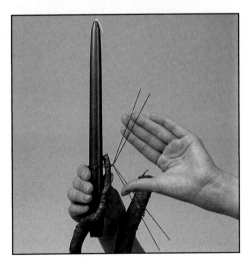

If you will be using candles, they must be securely fastened and it is equally essential that someone will be keeping an eye on them all the time that they are alight. It is also important when you add your flowers or plants to the tree to check that they will not be in the way of the flame. To attach candles, use two 0.71mm (22 gauge) wires, twisting the wires together to secure the candle to the branch. There should be at least three pairs of wires at the bottom of each candle, securing it to the branch.

SILVER LICHEN TREE

If you rapidly get bored with your Christmas tree and want something completely different for a New Year party, this is an ideal choice, as it is festive and at the same time unusual.

Find an interestingly-shaped branch that is covered in lichen; set it in a pot of plaster, and leave until dry. If you find a main branch/trunk that isn't quite the right shape you can always add or remove smaller branches where necessary. To add extra branches, wire them securely to the trunk with 1.25mm (18 gauge) stub wires. If they are small, they can be wired to one of the outer branches. Do make sure that all the added branches are firmly fixed in place, or you will find that they wobble about like a loose tooth!

Once you are pleased with the overall shape, you can add extra decorations and finishing touches. Here, I used artificial icicles and artificial fruit. (The icicles were in fact sold as catkins, but they looked much more like icicles to me, so that is what I have called them!) You will be able to find plastic or glass icicles at most Christmas decoration shops.

I also threaded some pearl beads over and through the branches, then added a few artificial stars. To finish, I sprinkled some silver rain over the bare parts of the branches.

PLANT TREE
WITH CANDLES

This highly dramatic tree is guaranteed to cause a sensation and is ideal for fireworks or bonfire celebrations.

Firstly set a large branch into a pot of plaster and leave to dry, then place in a large plant container and cover with a thick layer of soil. Now plant one or two large-leafed plants in the soil – arums, which I used here, have perfectly-shaped leaves and their red flowers complement this tree wonderfully. Attach three church candles to the branches, using 1.25mm (18 gauge) stub wires. It is essential that these are completely secure as otherwise they might slip and fall over, thereby causing a fire. It is not necessary to use candles but they do give a rather splendid effect. Water some maidenhair ferns very well, leave for about an hour, then take them out of their pots and wrap each root ball in plant wrap or strips of heavy-duty plastic before attaching them to the branches using 1.25mm (18 gauge) stub wires. If you spray the ferns frequently with a fine plant mister they should stay fresh for between three and four days.

STAR, MOON AND CATKIN TREE

Children's parties, Hallowe'en and bonfire nights are all ideal occasions for making this dramatic tree. To make this tree, start by choosing several contorted branches and set them all into one bucket of plaster. Once this has dried, add smaller branches of catkins, fixing them securely to the main branches with 1.25mm (18 gauge) stub wires.

To make the stars and moons, either use ready-covered cardboard or glue a sheet of gold paper to each side of a piece of heavy card and cut out the shapes, using a sharp stencil or a craft knife. If you are using a craft knife, you may find it best to make a template so that you can draw the shapes before cutting them out. Make a hole in one end of each shape – use a hole punch if you have one – then thread a length of thin nylon fishing line through each hole and use these to tie the shapes to the branches.

Instead of arranging fairy lights behind and around the base of the tree, as shown in the photograph, you might prefer to twine the lights around the actual branches of the tree.

WISTERIA TREE

If you want to decorate a stretch of wall, whether inside or out, why not make an instant flowering tree? If you choose artificial flowers, you could make a permanent display for a conservatory or an empty wall. Here, I used wisteria, but there are plenty of other artificial flowers, fruits and foliages that are equally suitable for this type of tree, including ivies, lilac, roses, grapes, clematis, forsythia and hydrangeas.

You do not, of course, have to use wisteria branches for the arrangement. Wisteria takes so long to grow that you would make yourself very unpopular if you did this. Instead, choose weathered branches of almost any type; you could even use gnarled, thick stems of ivy. You will find that it is easiest to pull away a stem that is growing along a fallen tree trunk. Wherever possible, use materials that are already dead, to avoid vandalizing a growing tree, but take care when choosing branches – they may be too rotten to use, and tend to harbour insects.

When making these larger constructed trees, you will have the greatest degree of scope with the shape if you construct your tree against a wall, which will enable you to wire the branches to the wall as well as to the main trunk of the tree. To make the tree, set the main branch into a pot of plaster, leave it to dry, and then wire on extra branches and artificial flowers.

GERBERA TREE

The bright colours and daisy-like shapes of gerberas make them a good choice for a large tree, as the flowers can be easily viewed and appreciated. When using gerberas in this way, you will find that they will last longer if you let them drink fresh water for at least a day, to condition them, before you start to arrange them.

It will also help if you wrap them in threes in tissue paper. To do this, take a sheet of tissue paper and, starting at one corner, roll it at an angle, making a long sausage shape. Flatten the roll, then take three flowers and wrap the tissue paper roll down the stem, starting as close to the heads as possible. Use a piece of tape to hold the roll in place. The effect is rather like a stiff collar, and will prevent the heads of the flowers from drooping before you are ready to use them.

Find an interestingly-shaped branch; set it into a pot of plaster, and leave it to dry. Soak two blocks of green oasis in water, then cut each one into three and wrap each piece separately and securely in wire netting. Wire these blocks on to the branches with 1.25mm (18 gauge) stub wires. As this can be rather messy it is best if, before you start work, you put down a plastic sheet covered with a dust sheet to collect the bits and protect the floor.

Water some pots of ivy well; leave them for about an hour, then remove the plants from their pots and wrap each root ball in plant wrap or heavy-duty plastic. Attach them to the branches, fixing them just behind the oasis blocks, with 1.25mm (18 gauge) stub wires. The trails of ivy can be used to conceal the blocks, once the gerberas have been arranged.

Arrange the gerberas in the oasis blocks, making sure that you do not push the stems in so far that they come out the other side of the oasis (this is easier than you might imagine!). It is obviously important that the stems should be in the oasis, or the flowers will very quickly die, whereas the tree should last for about three days.

As an extra decoration, you can cover the container in which the tree has been set with sphagnum moss. This is secured in place by wrapping black reel wire right around the container. The wire sinks into the moss and is therefore invisible.

EUCALYPTUS ARRANGEMENT

Long stems of eucalyptus, placed in a tall vase of water, make a large and very dramatic arrangement that will not only give off a marvellous scent but will also last for at least two weeks. It is not always easy to judge height from a photograph – this particular arrangement was about 3 metres (10 feet) tall. You do not need any real flower-arranging skills to create something like this, yet it will look stunning when finished, especially if it is placed by a large window or a light wall, against which the stems of foliage will stand out to their best advantage.

Begin by putting about five stems together in a vase and then, using these as a base, arrange the rest of the eucalyptus around them. You will need to insert many stems of eucalyptus to be able to arrange them in wire netting – the large number should be sufficient to prevent individual stems from flopping about. A large heavy vase, of the type that is sometimes used for umbrellas, is ideal, if you are lucky enough to possess one, but any large heavy container will be adequate as long as it is water-tight. If you are worried about the weight of the container, you can always put bricks or stones in the bottom.

This sort of effect can also be achieved with blossom branches, silver birch, catkins, cotoneaster, copper beech or any other suitable foliages. This means that the basic arrangement can be adapted for different times of the year and, if the foliage is altered, can even be used in high summer, perhaps without the fairy lights. A sprinkling of fairy lights adds a party atmosphere to the arrangement, however, but take great care to ensure that they are held well clear of the water – you don't want to electrocute your guests!

Be careful, when taking such large branches, that you do not damage the tree irreparably. Stand back from the living tree and take a good look at its shape to see where it could helpfully be pruned. A useful gadget to borrow for this exercise would be a long-armed pruner.

If the arrangement is to continue to look its best, and especially if it is kept in a centrally-heated room, the water in the vase will have to be renewed frequently and topped up. This is ideally a two-person job, as the arrangement will have to be lifted out of the vase, and one person will have to hold it together while the other quickly changes the water, which will weigh quite heavily.

Large collections of foliage or flowers, arranged in this manner, are perfect for big, empty entertainment rooms, as they will fill up a corner or an area of undecorated wall. This is probably one of the cheapest and most dramatic ways of decorating a large empty space.

USEFUL TIPS

Christmas trees

With Christmas trees, as with so many other things, you have to pay a high price to get the best quality. Whether this is money well spent, only you can decide. If your tree is only expected to last for the standard twelve days of Christmas, it may not be necessary to buy a particularly good one. If, on the other hand, you want a long-lasting tree, I find that the best variety is blue pine, often known as Noble Fir. This has an attractive colour and a chunky, well-covered appearance. It is not always readily available, in which case my second choice would be Normandia.

We start selling our trees in the middle of November, and find that they keep very well outside. It is only when trees come inside that they start to lose their needles. As well-shaped trees tend to be bought up very quickly, it makes sense to buy early and store your tree outside. It is silly to wait until the last possible moment, by which time you will find that most of the standard heights have sold out, and you will be forced to choose between a dwarf, a giant, or a lop-sided, mangy tree, which has to be carefully pruned.

Holly

This only lasts for a short time – about a week – indoors, and it is usually very difficult to find holly with berries by the time Christmas arrives, as the birds will have taken them. For this reason, it is a good idea to buy a few artificial holly berries.

(Mind you, I have a horrid vision of blazing artificial berries on a Christmas pudding!)

Before using holly, it is a good idea to condition it like any other foliage. Cut the ends and then bash them with a hammer; put the sprigs into a bucket of water, and leave them to drink for at least 24 hours before using them. This applies to all foliages and blossoms.

Watering

One reason why Christmas arrangements tend to look a little tired at the end of the season is because people forget to water them. If you water your green oasis decorations at least once a day, they should survive much longer. Spray door wreaths from time to time with a mister to keep them fresh.

Storing dried and artificial flowers

When storing dried flowers, perhaps during the summer, put them in a large cardboard box, to protect them from dust, and keep them in a dry place, such as an attic. The same applies to arrangements in baskets, which again should be stored in a box, perhaps with tissue paper around it. Mark the box carefully – it is amazing how other people will unerringly put your precious box of dried flowers at the bottom of a pile of heavy objects, or will casually turn it upside down.

Before storing artificial garlanding, remove any extra decorations and fold the garland as flat as you can before packing it.

INDEX

Apples and nightlights	106	Iron trees	16
Artificial garland	39	Kumquat garland	35
Autumn tree	86	Lace and lights tree	20
Bare branch tree	129	Larch twigs in a tank	118
Bonfire basket	126	Lavender tree	85
Blue and burgundy basket	115	Lichen tree with glass baubles	80
Blue and pink tree	22	Midsummer splendour	120
Burgundy tree	18	Miniature trees	66
Carousel advent ring	99	Mistletoe ball	92
Champagne garland	31	Mistletoe table	102
Christmas basket	32	Moss tree	81
Christmas candle	95	Napkin garland	32
Christmas door wreath	52	Partridge in a pear tree	61
Christmas pine garland	29	Peach bow tree	19
Covered basket	28	Pine and nut balls	56
Dried garland	40	Pine and tartan tree	68
Easter garland	34	Pine cone tree	88
Edelweiss and poppy head tree	84	Pink and cream arrangement	111
Eucalyptus arrangement	141	Pink and pearl tree	70
Floral candlestick	100	Pink tree	90
Fresh floral arrangement	114	Plant tree with candles	134
Fruit and flower tree	68	Protea tree	82
Flower, fruit and candle		Red and green tree	14
arrangement	101	Sandy arrangement	124
Fruit garland	42	Shamrock tree	89
Fruit plaque	57	Silver lichen tree	132
Fruit pyramid	74	Small yellow tree	86
Garlanded fireplace	44	Small white tree	72
Gerbera tree	138	Star, moon and catkin tree	135
German gingerbread tree	64	Summer artificial wreath	50
Gold and frosty tree	11	Summery garland	38
Golden advent ring	105	Tartan table design	108
Gypsophila ball	77	Valentine heart	59
Hanging maypole decoration	51	Vegetable garland	36
Hanging pine advent ring	53	Violet garland	25
Harvest arrangement	116	Winter basket	124
Harvest wreath	47	Winter fireplace arrangement	55
Holly advent ring	104	Winter tree	82
Holly and nuts table decoration	98	Winter velvet	116
Hydrangea and peony tree	72	Wisteria tree	137
Hydrangea garland	30	Yellow and white basket	122

AUTHOR'S ACKNOWLEDGMENTS

Thank you, Topher, for your extraordinary patience and for all your love.

My very special thanks to:

Katharine Bull, Annabel Lutyens, Karen Flindall, Hannah Catling, Lucy Blanchard, Francis Bearman, Cherry Clark, Donna Henderson, Caroline Little, Tanya Lugli, Angus Pelletier

Paul, Caroline and Clements Van den Boogaard for the loan of their wonderful home

Major Fenwick, Mrs Dormer and all the Chelsea Gardener staff for the loan of Christmas decorations and for all their help

Barbara Stewart for her creative styling and advice

Jon Stewart for his wonderful photographs

Kay Small for her assistance with the photography

Jane Struthers for all her hard work and great humour

Second Nature Ltd, 10 Malton Road, London W10, for the loan of their Christmas decorations

A & S Designs Ltd, 237 Acton Lane, London W4, for the loan of pine cone wreaths and baskets

David at John Austin, Stand M5, 305 Flower Market, New Covent Garden, London SW8, for the wonderful fresh flowers

Charlie Gardiner, 302/303 Flower Market, New Covent Garden, London SW8, for the wonderful fresh flowers

A & F Bacon, 354 Flower Market, New Covent Garden, London SW8, for the wonderful foliage

Best Blooms Ltd, Cheapside House, Buckhurst Road, Ascot, Berkshire, for the amazing artificial flowers

Austin & Co., 12 Sandiford Road, Sutton, Surrey, for the marvellous artificial flowers

Cockerel's, 313/314 Flower Market, New Covent Garden Market, London SW8, for sundry items

Veevers-Carter Flowers are at:

The Chelsea Gardener, 125 Sydney Street, London SW3 6NR.
Tel: 071 352 7658

150 Old Brompton Road, London SW5 0BE. Tel: 071 370 0549